THE TASTES OF CALIFORNIA WINE COUNTRY
NAPA/SONOMA

A Restaurant Guide & Restaurant Recipe Cookbook

A Bed & Breakfast Guide
& Bed & Breakfast Recipe Cookbook

Written & Compiled by Sonnie Imes

*To Robin: Without whose help this
book would have been almost impossible,
and not nearly as much fun.*

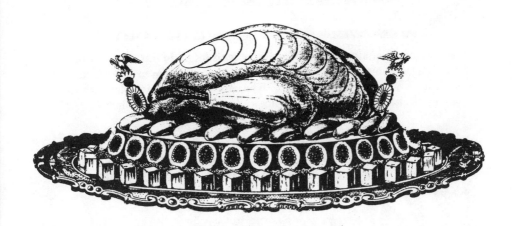

Buena Vista

PRIVATE RESERVE

CARNEROS

Cabernet Sauvignon

ESTATE GROWN AND BOTTLED BY
BUENA VISTA WINERY, CARNEROS, SONOMA, CALIFORNIA, USA
Alcohol 13.0% by Volume

The consistent quality and rich Carneros fruit found in this wine continues Buena Vista's long-established reputation for excellence in producing award-winning Cabernet Sauvignon wines. The wine is deep red in color with rich flavors of cherry, black currant, spice and cedar followed by slight hints of chocolate.

Enjoy this wine at room temperature served with beef bourguignonne, barbequed London broil or venison stew. For a special treat, complement dark (bittersweet) chocolate desserts with a glass of Cabernet Sauvignon from Buena Vista Winery.

Buena Vista Winery

18000 Old Winery Road, Sonoma, California

Open daily 10:00 a.m. to 5:00 p.m. for wine tasting and tours. We also invite you to visit our Presshouse Gallery, showcasing a rich diversity of artistic talent, and to join us for a variety of cultural events including Mozart and Shakespeare.

FOR INFORMATION, PLEASE CALL (707)938-8504

Table of Contents

3

Pasta Alfredo with Fettucini
Chicken Duexelle
Bread Pudding

11 La Gare 85
   Duck Pate'
   Prawns Bordelaise
   Tournedos de Boeuf a l'estragon
   Riz de Veau Financiere

12 La Province 91
   Chicken or Veal Marsala
   Beef Bourguignone
   Red Snapper Tarragon

13 Le Rhone 95
   Adube a la Cote du Rhone Red
   Gateau Normand Apple Cake
   Glace Royale

14 Madrona Manor 99
   Bran Muffins
   Sour Cream Vegetable Salad
   Garlic Mashed Potatoes
   Marmalade
   Soupirs de nonnes (Nun's Sighs) or Churros
   Pumpkin Chiffon Pie

15 Main Street Bar & Grill 107
   Fried Cheese and Zucchini
   Cajun-Style Linguini
   Grilled Chicken Breast with
      Sun-Dried Tomato Pesto
   Gaspacho Sorbet with Garden Vegetables

16 Marshall House 113
   Sauerbraten
   Sauerbraten Gravy

Oysters on the Half Shell with
        Spicy California Dipping Sauce
Spicy California Dipping Sauce
Fresh Pasta with Italian Sausage &
        a Rainbow of Peppers
Hot Radicchio Salad with Pancetta and Chevre
Fruit Gratin

Bed & Breakfast Inns

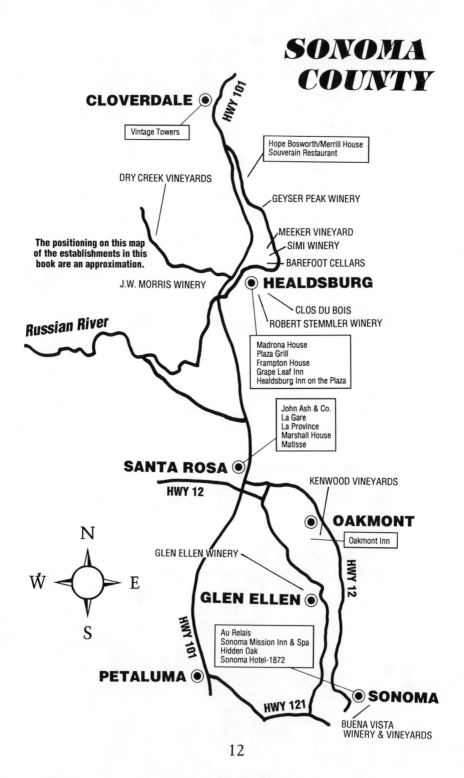

SONOMA COUNTY

CLOVERDALE ⊙

HWY 101

Vintage Towers

Hope Bosworth/Merrill House
Souverain Restaurant

DRY CREEK VINEYARDS

GEYSER PEAK WINERY

MEEKER VINEYARD

SIMI WINERY

BAREFOOT CELLARS

The positioning on this map
of the establishments in this
book are an approximation.

J.W. MORRIS WINERY

HEALDSBURG ⊙

CLOS DU BOIS

ROBERT STEMMLER WINERY

Russian River

Madrona House
Plaza Grill
Frampton House
Grape Leaf Inn
Healdsburg Inn on the Plaza

John Ash & Co.
La Gare
La Province
Marshall House
Matisse

SANTA ROSA ⊙

HWY 12

KENWOOD VINEYARDS

OAKMONT ⊙

Oakmont Inn

GLEN ELLEN WINERY

HWY 12

N
W · E
S

GLEN ELLEN ⊙

HWY 101

Au Relais
Sonoma Mission Inn & Spa
Hidden Oak
Sonoma Hotel-1872

PETALUMA ⊙

SONOMA ⊙

HWY 121

BUENA VISTA
WINERY & VINEYARDS

12

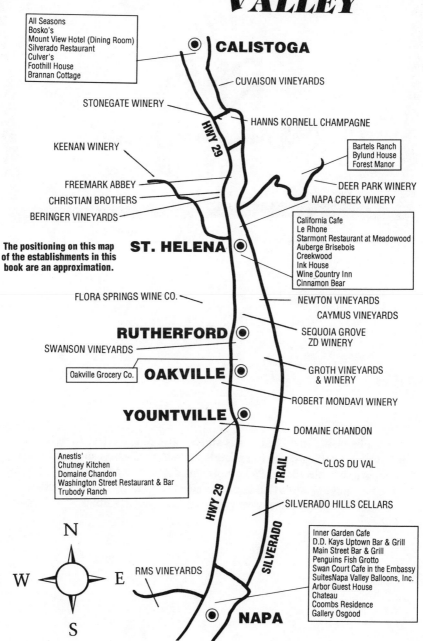

NAPA VALLEY

All Seasons
Bosko's
Mount View Hotel (Dining Room)
Silverado Restaurant
Culver's
Foothill House
Brannan Cottage

CALISTOGA

CUVAISON VINEYARDS

STONEGATE WINERY

HWY 29

HANNS KORNELL CHAMPAGNE

KEENAN WINERY

Bartels Ranch
Bylund House
Forest Manor

FREEMARK ABBEY

DEER PARK WINERY

CHRISTIAN BROTHERS

NAPA CREEK WINERY

BERINGER VINEYARDS

California Cafe
Le Rhone
Starmont Restaurant at Meadowood
Auberge Brisebois
Creekwood
Ink House
Wine Country Inn
Cinnamon Bear

The positioning on this map
of the establishments in this
book are an approximation.

ST. HELENA

FLORA SPRINGS WINE CO.

NEWTON VINEYARDS

CAYMUS VINEYARDS

RUTHERFORD

SEQUOIA GROVE
ZD WINERY

SWANSON VINEYARDS

Oakville Grocery Co.

OAKVILLE

GROTH VINEYARDS
& WINERY

ROBERT MONDAVI WINERY

YOUNTVILLE

DOMAINE CHANDON

Anestis'
Chutney Kitchen
Domaine Chandon
Washington Street Restaurant & Bar
Trubody Ranch

TRAIL

CLOS DU VAL

HWY 29

SILVERADO HILLS CELLARS

SILVERADO

N
W   E
S

RMS VINEYARDS

Inner Garden Cafe
D.D. Kays Uptown Bar & Grill
Main Street Bar & Grill
Penguins Fish Grotto
Swan Court Cafe in the Embassy
SuitesNapa Valley Balloons, Inc.
Arbor Guest House
Chateau
Coombs Residence
Gallery Osgood

NAPA

In September 1982, RMS Vineyards started distilling its first Alambic brandy in Napa, California. Select premium California wines such as French Colombard, Chenin Blanc, Pinot Noir, Palomino, and Muscat are specially made for double distillation and then slowly and individually distilled in small French copper pot stills know as "Alambics."

Restaurants

N E W T O N

CHARDONNAY
NAPA VALLEY

Produced and Bottled by Newton Vineyard St Helena Napa Valley Ca Alc 12.5% by Vol Contains Sulfites

Whenever we have guests at Newton Vineyard, we serve them this special chicken dish. Delicious with Newton Chardonnay.

NEWTON CHICKEN SALAD WITH PEANUT BUTTER DRESSING (Serves 4)

4 breasts of chicken (skinned)	½ lb. of cherry tomatoes
1 pint chicken stock	1 large cucumber

Poach chicken in stock. Remove from stock and allow to cool. Cut into julienne strips. Serve on a bed of thinly sliced cucumber, garnished with the cherry tomatoes. Top with peanut butter dressing.

Peanut Butter Dressing

½ jar of peanut butter	1 finely chopped spring onion
1 fluid oz. soya bean extract	1 tablespoon Worcestershire sauce
1 teaspoon each: paprika, cayenne	Juice of one lemon
pepper, garlic powder	½ cup of finely chopped parsley

Mix all ingredients together to form a thick paste. Add water slowly until sauce consistency is reached. Sprinkle parsley on top.

16

ALL SEASONS

1400 Lincoln • Calistoga, California
(707) 942-9111
Hours: 9:00 a.m. - 9:00 p.m., Daily
Lunch, Every day
Brunch on Weekends
Thursday-Monday, Dinner
Credit Cards: Visa, M/C, A/X
Prices: Inexpensive-Moderate
Reservations: Suggested for 6 or more
Specialties: Bistro Cooking

Homemade pasta, desserts, specialty smoked meats and a full deli market all add up to All Seasons Cafe in Calistoga. Daily lunch specials range from fresh fish, soup, sandwiches, pizza and pasta to complement the regular lunch menu of subs and fresh salads. With a predominance of California wines, All Seasons has over 1400 wines available to choose from and 20 premium wines by the taste, glass or bottle, changing bi-weekly. There is also a large variety of domestic and imported beers and several non-alcoholic grape juices as well. You'll feel a definite European flavor and flair in the presentation and preparation at All Seasons, with prices in the inexpensive to moderate range.

17

Black Bean Soup

3 c. black beans
5 c. water
2 Serano chilies, chopped
1 onion, sliced
4 cloves garlic, minced
2 T. olive oil
8 c. chicken stock
2 bay leaves
1½ T. cumin
1 orange peel

Soak black beans in water overnight; drain next morning. Saute Serrano chilis (or milder chili pepper), onion and garlic in olive oil until onions are transluscent. Add drained beans and chicken stock and season with bay leaves, cumin and orange peel. Cook the beans until they are tender; puree, add salt to taste. If soup is too thick, thin with orange juice. Garnish with sour cream and chopped cilantro.

Chocolate Macadamia and Caramel Tarte

For the pastry shell (one 9" fluted tarte pan):
6 oz. cold butter, cut in small cubes
2½ c. flour
¼ c. sugar
⅛ t. salt
1 egg

In electric mixer with paddle, mix the butter, flour, sugar and salt until butter is pea-sized and coated with flour mixture, or cut these ingredients in with two knives. Add egg and mix until all comes together as a dough. Roll out to ¼" thickness and form into a 9" tarte pan; chill. Prick the bottom in several places with a fork. Bake at 375° for 18 minutes. Set aside to cool.

Caramel Filling:
½ c. sugar
½ c. dark Karo syrup
2 oz. butter
1 c. heavy cream

Place first three ingredients and ½ c. heavy cream in a heavy saucepan with a candy thermometer, stirring until sugar is dissolved. Cook until thermometer is 244°. Remove from heat. Stir in remaining ½ c. heavy cream. Cook again until temperature reaches 230°. Remove the mixture to a clean bowl and cool completely.

Chocolate Macadamia and Caramel Torte (Cont.)

The Macadamia Nuts:

Roast a scant two cups of macadamia nuts at 375° on a cookie sheet for approximately ten minutes. Halfway through the cooking time, rotate the pan and stir the nuts. Watch them carefully the last few minutes.

Chocolate Topping:
3 oz. heavy cream
¼ c. sugar
1½ t. light Karo syrup
1½ T. butter

3 oz. finely chopped semi-sweet chocolate

Stir together the first four ingredients until hot; then add the chocolate and stir until completely melted. Set aside.

To Assemble:

Reserve a small amount of caramel to make a spiral design on the finished tarte. Spread the rest of the caramel carefully into the bottom of the baked pastry shell. Coarsely chop the macadamia nuts and press into the caramel. Spread the chocolate glaze smoothly over the caramel and nut layers. Refrigerate for 15 minutes to set the chocolate glaze. Place the reserved caramel in a pastry bag with a small round tip. Starting in the middle of the tarte, pipe out a thin spiral design. With the back of a paring knife, draw lines from the center to the edge of the tarte. which "pulls" gently at the caramel threads and makes a lovely finishing touch. Serve at room temperature.

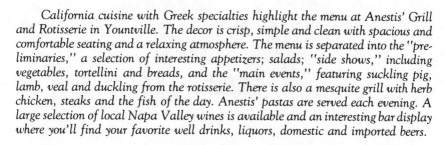

ANESTIS'
GRILL & ROTISSERIE

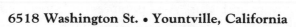

6518 Washington St. • Yountville, California
(707) 944-1500
Hours: 9:00 a.m. - 12:00 p.m., Breakfast, Sat. & Sun.
12:00 p.m. - 5:00 p.m., Lunch, Sat. & Sun.
5:00 p.m. - 10:00 p.m., Dinner, Mon. - Sun.
11:30 a.m. - 3:00 p.m., Lunch, Mon. - Fri.
Credit Cards: Visa, M/C, A/X, D/C
Prices: Moderate
Reservations: Suggested
Specialties: California Cuisine with Greek Specialties

California cuisine with Greek specialties highlight the menu at Anestis' Grill and Rotisserie in Yountville. The decor is crisp, simple and clean with spacious and comfortable seating and a relaxing atmosphere. The menu is separated into the "preliminaries," a selection of interesting appetizers; salads; "side shows," including vegetables, tortellini and breads, and the "main events," featuring suckling pig, lamb, veal and duckling from the rotisserie. There is also a mesquite grill with herb chicken, steaks and the fish of the day. Anestis' pastas are served each evening. A large selection of local Napa Valley wines is available and an interesting bar display where you'll find your favorite well drinks, liquors, domestic and imported beers.

21

Greek Pate of Red Caviar
(Taramosalata)

½ c. Tarama (Red Greek Caviar) *
6 lbs. potatoes (pared & cooked)
1 c. olive oil
¼ c. fresh lemon juice
1 T. onion juice
1 T. white wine

Put Tarama in food processor with small amount of oil, lemon juice, onion juice and whip. Add potatoes and slowly add the remaining oil, lemon juice, onion juice and wine. Refrigerate for 3 hours before serving. Served with croutons, crackers or french bread as appetizers.

Yield: about 1 quart

* Available in Greek delicatessens

Whipped Garlic Potato with Garlic - Allioli

One head of garlic (peeled)
6 lbs. potatoes (cooked)
1 c. olive oil
⅓ c. white wine vinegar
1 T. white table wine
1 egg yolk
pinch of white pepper
1 t. salt

Clean garlic and chop finely. Clean potatoes and cut into quarters, strain water, then mash. Put garlic and potatoes into a food processor and whip. Add salt and pepper, slowly add oil, vinegar and wine until all these ingredients are slowly mixed. Add 1 egg yolk and mix for 5 minutes. Refrigerate for 2 hours before serving. Served with broiled fish, chicken or broiled eggplant.

Yield: about 1 quart

Yogurt Garlic Sauce (Tsatsiki)

6 cloves garlic
16 oz. sour cream
8 oz. plain yogurt
2 cucumbers (pared, shredded & strained)
     (make sure there are no seeds)
4 T. olive oil
1 T. white wine vinegar
1 T. white wine
1 t. salt
pinch of white pepper
1 t. dill weed

Mix all ingredients together and refrigerate for 2 hours. Serve as a topping for stuffed grape leaves with rice or use as a dip for vegetables.

Yield: 4 cups

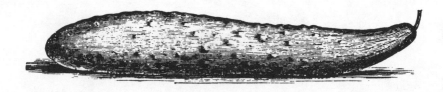

Au Relais Restaurant

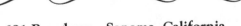

691 Broadway • Sonoma, California
(707) 996-1031
Hours: 11:00 a.m. - 10:00 p.m., Every Day
Sometimes closed for Holidays in Dec., Jan. or Feb.
Credit Cards: Visa, M/C, A/X
Prices: Moderate
Reservations: Suggested on Weekends
Specialties: French Continental with Mediterranean Flair

This elegant French country restaurant with dining inside and out has won the praises of food critics over the years with its innovative cuisine, four-star Mobil rating and consistently excellent food. Au Relais has also received the prestigious Holiday Award, making it one of only 360 restaurants in the U.S., Mexico and Canada to be bestowed with this honor. Complementing the Au Relais Restaurant is the Au Relais Bed and Breakfast Inn with five luxurious rooms in shades of rose. The inn operates much like a local tourist center, channeling visitors to the finest restaurants, wineries and entertainment in the valley.

Cold Cucumber & Spinach Soup

1 onion
1 large potato
1 leek
3 sprigs fresh parsley
1 T. butter
1½ pt. water or chicken stock
2 cubes chicken boullion
salt and pepper
½ bunch blanched spinach
2 peeled cucumbers, chopped
½ c. sour cream
1 T. mayonnaise
1 t. horseradish
juice of 2 lemons
2 drops tabasco
1 avocado (optional)

Peel, wash and chop roughly onion, potato, leek and parsley.
Place in saucepan with 1 T. of butter and saute lightly for 5 minutes covered. Add 1½ pt. water or chicken stock; boil for 20
minutes. Let cool and blend. Add boullion, salt and pepper to
taste. Blend in remaining ingredients, adding salt and pepper to
taste. Add avocado at last minute just before serving (adds a nice
touch).

Serves 5

Zucchini Soup

1 leek
2 stalks celery
½ onion
1 oz. butter
1 oz. flour
2 pt. chicken stock
5 medium zucchini, diced
1 c. heavy cream
salt and pepper to taste
1 whole zucchini

Wash and dice leek, celery and onion. Saute very lightly in butter and flour and make into a paste. Moisten with the chicken stock and bring to a boil. Add diced zucchini; boil for 10 minutes. Puree in a food processor and add heavy cream, salt and pepper. Grate whole zucchini into the mixture.

Garlic-Toasted
French Cheese Bread

1 loaf French bread
10 cloves garlic
olive oil
2 oz. dry imported (or domestic) goat cheese, grated
2 oz. imported French Roquefort cheese, grated
good quality Greek black olives
1 T. herbes de provence
1 T. chopped parsley
1 T. chopped walnuts

Split French bread lengthwise and toast in hot oven. Rub bread with whole cloves of garlic, then sprinkle with olive oil. Mix cheeses with black olives, herbs, parsley and walnuts. Coat bread and bake in a hot oven until cheese is melted.

Serves 6

Chicken Gloria

salt and pepper to taste
½ c. flour
2 chicken legs
2 chicken breasts, boned
1 T. butter
½ c. sherry
½ c. heavy cream
½ c. crushed walnuts
1 doz. apricot halves and juice

Season and flour the chicken pieces. Saute (skin side down) lightly in butter in a saute pan. Bake in a 400° oven for 10 minutes. Turn and bake another 5 minutes. Pour off the fat. Deglaze* with sherry. Add cream, nuts and apricots immediately. Bake 5 to 8 minutes, basting the chicken with the sauce. Serve immediately.

Serves 4

* See Glossary

Pork Dijonaise

1 lb. pork scallopini* or pork chops**
1 T. butter
2 chopped shallots
2 cloves garlic, minced
12 cornichons, julienned
½ c. dry white wine
½ c. heavy cream
2 T. Dijon mustard
1 T. chopped parsley or cilantro

After the scallopini are sauted on both sides (or chops are cooked nearly done), pour off any excess fat. In a saute pan over high flame add a pat of butter to the pork. Toss in shallots, garlic, and saute for 10 seconds. Add cornichons and white wine. It will sizzle around pan, and the juices will deglace. Let the wine boil away quickly, then add the cream and Dijon mustard. The sauce will come together. Place pork in a serving dish and pour the sauce over it. Serve with chopped parsley or cilantro.

Serves 4

* Pork scallopini must be sauteed quickly on top of the stove.

** Pork chops should be sauteed on top of the stove and then finished in the oven (length of time varies).

Cassoulet Maison

1 lb. cubed lamb
1 lb. cubed pork
½ lb. smoked bacon
1 lb. navy beans, soaked overnight
1 carrot
1 leek
1 stalk celery
1 onion
1 T. oil
6 cloves garlic
4 T. tomato paste
mixed herbs
2 garlic sausages
1 roast duck or smoked goose
1 tomato, diced
1 c. fresh bread crumbs

Saute all meats until golden brown; drain off fat. Blanch* navy beans and drain. Wash and cube all vegetables. Melt oil in a large braising pan and saute lightly all vegetables and garlic. Mix in all meat, tomato paste, beans and herbs. Moisten with water and braise approximately 1½ to 2 hours. When cooked, place in individual casserole dishes or one large one. In layers, add sliced sausage, smoked goose or duck and fresh diced tomato on top. Moisten with a little white wine if necessary. Scatter fresh bread crumbs on top. Bake in a moderate oven ½ hour just before serving.

* See Glossary

Paella Valenciana

1 large fryer chicken (cut up)
8 prawns
8 scampi
1 lb. octopus meat
1 lobster
1 lb. chorizo sausage
8 clams or mussels (or combination)
1 lb. white fish
1 lb. red mullet
8 oz. baby shrimp
1 bell pepper
2 stalks celery
1 onion
3 cloves garlic
2 tomatoes
¼ lb. green beans
1 T. oil
1 lb. rice
1 c. chicken stock
pinch of saffron
fine herbs and bay leaf

Dice first 6 ingredients and saute in hot oil. Add rice and saute 5 more minutes. Arrange the remaining ingredients, plus sauted vegetables and rice (except for chicken stock, saffron, fine herbs, and bay leaf) in a flat 3-inch deep paella pot. Boil chicken stock with saffron and herbs. Pour stock over paella and bake in a 400° oven for approximately 45 minutes. Serve in the paella pot.

Serves a bunch

Chocolate Mousse

8 oz. sugar
4 oz. flour
8 egg yolks
1 pt. milk
8 oz. chocolate
½ oz. gelatin
1 pt. whipping cream
8 egg whites

Beat together sugar, flour and egg yolks. Boil milk and pour into the beaten mixture, thus making a custard. Melt chocolate and add to mixture. Melt gelatin in a little water and add to the chocolate custard and let it cool. Beat the whipping cream; beat the egg whites until they form a stiff meringue. When chocolate custard is cool and almost setting, fold in the whipping cream quickly, then the meringue. Pour into a mold and let it set.

Serves 8

Keenan

Estate
Napa Valley Chardonnay

Grown, Produced and Bottled by
Robert Keenan Winery, Spring Mt., St. Helena, Ca.
ALCOHOL 13.0% BY VOLUME

Elegant and austere; crisp with acid and mildly oaked.

**Enhances oysters on the half shell, mesquite-grilled
fresh stripped bass and sole florentine.**

BOSKO'S
Ristorante
Est. 1983

1403 Lincoln Avenue • Calistoga, California
(707) 942-9088
Hours: 11:00 a.m. - 10:00 p.m., Daily
Credit Cards: None
Prices: Inexpensive-Moderate
Reservations: None
Specialties: Pasta

Everything from the brick walls, sawdust floor and delightful aroma of Italian cooking adds to the charm of Boskos, a fun place to meet friends and treat yourself to great Italian favorites. The soups and salads are nearly meals in themselves - a spoon stands stright up in a bowl of Bosko's homemade minestrone! Food is served at your table once you place your order at the counter in a cafeteria-style manner. Some 13 pasta salads make choosing difficult, and one is always vegetarian for those who prefer it. Or try one of the house specialties - Piacere, a linguini dish with a spicy white wine sauce, shrimp and clams. There is also a large selection of imported and domestic beers, plus a full wine list. To top it off, try one of Bosko's desserts - if you have room!

Quattro Stagione

⅓ c. red pepper, diced
⅓ c. green pepper, diced
½ c. red onion, diced
½ c. prosciutto, julienned
1½ oz. olive oil
1½ oz. clarified butter*
¼ t. oregano
¼ t. basil
1 pinch salt
2 pinches pepper
1 T. garlic, minced
5 oz. fresh pasta
⅓ c. Romano cheese

Saute peppers, onion and prosciutto in oil and butter and add oregano, basil, salt and pepper for approximatley 1½ minutes. Add garlic and cook for 15 seconds longer. Toss in 5 oz. fusilli (pasta), add cheese and serve.

Serves 1

* See Glossary

36

Glorioso

1½ oz. clarified butter
1½ oz. olive oil
4½ oz. sliced mushrooms
pinch of salt
2 pinches pepper
¼ t. red pepper flakes
1 heaping T. garlic, minced
5 oz. fresh pasta shells, cooked
⅓ c. Romano cheese

Heat butter and oil in saute pan. Add mushrooms, salt, pepper and red pepper flakes. Saute until mushrooms are soft. Add garlic and cook for 1 minute longer. Add pasta and toss with Romano cheese.

Serves 1

Italian Scallion

4 oz. scallions
1 oz. clarified butter *
1 oz. olive oil
2 pinches pepper
1 pinch salt
1 T. garlic, minced
7 oz. cream
6 oz. cooked pasta shells
1/3 c. Romano cheese

Saute scallions in butter and oil; add pepper and salt. After scallions have cooked for 1 minute; add garlic; toss. Add cream and reduce to a thick sauce. Add cooked pasta and Romano cheese and toss well.

Serves 1

* See Glossary

Piacere

2 t. clarified butter *
1½ T. chopped shallots
1½ T. chopped garlic
½ t. red pepper flakes
1 t. oregano
1 t. black pepper
½ c. white wine
4¾ c. clam juice
5 t. clarified butter *
⅔ c. flour
3 oz. olive oil
¼ lb. butter
3 c. chopped clams
1 t. pepper
1½ c. white wine
1 lb. bay shrimp

Melt 2 t. clarified butter and saute shallots, garlic, red pepper flakes, oregano and black pepper for 3 minutes. Add white wine and cook for 2 minutes at a boil. Add clam juice and bring to a boil. In a small pan, melt 5 t. clarified butter and add flour. Cook for 1 minute and add to boiling clam juice. Saute in ¼ lb. butter and olive oil, chopped clams, pepper, 1½ c. white wine and the shrimp. Cook for 5 minutes and combine all ingredients. Mix well and serve over linguini.

Serves 6-8

Chocolate Cheesecake

1 pack Nabisco Famous Chocolate Wafers
1½ t. cinnamon
2½ T. melted butter
1 c. sugar
2½ t. cocoa powder
½ c. Amaretto
1½ t. vanilla extract
1½ lb. cream cheese, softened
8½ oz. dark chocolate, melted
1 c. sour cream
3 eggs

Mix chocolate wafers and cinnamon in food processor. Add melted butter and mix again. Butter an 8-inch springform pan and empty ground wafers into it. Spread evenly and press down to form crust. Chill for 15 minutes. In processor, mix sugar, cocoa powder, Amaretto and vanilla. Add softened cream cheese and mix for 3 minutes. Pour into large mixing bowl. In processor, mix melted chocolate, sour cream and 3 eggs. Mix for 3 minutes. Add to cream cheese mixture and whip. Pour into springform pan and bake at 350° for 45 minutes.

Serves 12

3111 No. St. Helena Hwy. • St. Helena, California
In the Cement Works
(707) 963-5300
Hours: Every day, Lunch
Saturday & Sunday, Brunch
Every day, Dinner
Credit Cards: Visa, M/C, A/X
Prices: Moderate
Reservations: Suggested
Specialties: New American Cuisine

You won't find anything frozen at the California Cafe - everything here is fresh - from the seafood to the homemade pasta. Specializing in new American cuisine, this restaurant also boasts a delicious mesquite grill selection, as well as daily specials and game dishes. Over 60 Napa Valley wines are available to choose from and you can enjoy a lovely vineyard setting as you dine on the patio. Service is friendly and attentive and there are many items to tempt your taste buds on the menu.

41

Cafe Caesar Salad Dressing

3 egg yolks
¼ c. chopped garlic
¼ oz. tabasco
1¾ oz. anchovies
2 t. dry mustard
1½ c. olive oil
½ c. lemon juice
¾ c. red wine vinegar
1½ c. corn oil
¼ c. plus 2 T. parmesan cheese
dash of black pepper

Place egg yolks, garlic, tabasco, anchovies and dry mustard in food processor and whip. Drizzle in olive oil slowly until thick. Add lemon juice and wine vinegar, alternately with corn oil. Add parmesan cheese and black pepper.

Makes about 5 cups

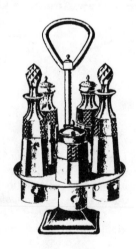

Veal and Duck Liver Pate´

1¾ lb. veal
1¾ lb. smoked chicken or pork butt
1 lb. duck livers
2 lb. bacon to line pan with
bay leaves to line with
½ t. thyme
½ t. white pepper
½ t. salt
4 eggs
½ c. cognac
½ c. shallots
¼ c. garlic
¼ t. allspice

Grind all ingredients through fine grinder 3 times. Line loaf pan with bacon and bay leaves. Fill with mixture and bake at 350° in water bath for approximately 1¼-1½ hours or to 140° internal temperature. Chill thoroughly before slicing.

Makes 9" loaf pan

Poached King Salmon with Champagne Sauce & Kiwis

1 pat butter
4 7-oz. Bodega Bay King Salmon filets
½ bottle dry champagne
dash of lemon juice
salt and white pepper
2 c. extra heavy cream
¼ lb. sweet butter
2 fresh, firm kiwis, sliced

Lightly coat medium saute pan with small amount of sweet butter. Place salmon filets ½ inch apart; cover with champagne, dash of lemon juice and salt and pepper. Cover, bring to full boil, ignite alcohol, reduce to low simmer and add cream. Cook until fish is barely done. Transfer fish to warmed plates. Reduce cream mixture until slightly thickened; whisk butter in, piece by piece, until thick. Pour sauce over fish; garnish with kiwi.

Serves 4

Grilled Marinated Pork Chops

Marinade:
1 c. pineapple juice
¼ c. rice wine vinegar
1 c. soy sauce
⅛ c. pureed fresh ginger
¼ c. chopped fresh cilantro
½ c. fresh chopped pineapple
½ c. water

16 pork chops (approximately 7 oz. each)

Combine all marinade ingredients. Marinate center-cut pork chops for at least 3 hours or up to 2 days. To grill chops, lightly oil them and grill over hot mesquite charcoals until medium-done (approximately 4-5 minutes on each side). Garnish with homemade apple sauce (recipe follows).

Serves 8

Apple Sauce

10 green apples (preferably Sebastopol Gravensteins)
1 oz. sweet butter
½ c. white wine
½ c. pure maple syrup
¼ c. brandy
cinnamon, nutmeg & mace, to taste

Saute apples in butter until carmelized; add white wine, bring to rapid boil, stirring constantly for 5 minutes. Add all other ingredients. Mix until incorporated. Serve warm.

Serves 8

California Fruit Tart

Tart Shell:
1 c. softened butter (unsalted)
2 c. all-purpose flour
½ c. sugar
1 c. chopped, toasted almonds

Filling:
1 8-oz. pkg. cream cheese
⅓ c. sugar
2 eggs
2 T. lemon juice
2 t. grated orange peel

Coating:
Use top-quality Apricot Tart Nappage or Pie Glaze*

Press dough into French tart pan that has been coated with non-stick spray. Weight with parchment and beans; pre-bake for 20 minutes at 350°. Remove beans and cool. Mix all custard (filling) ingredients in food processor. Pour in shell and bake ½ hour at 350° or until custard is cooked. Cool; slice fresh seasoned fruits and arrange in concentric circle. Glaze is optional.

Serves 10-12

* Available in specialty stores.

ROUND HILL

CABERNET SAUVIGNON

NAPA VALLEY

Produced and Bottled by Round Hill Vineyards
St. Helena, California, Alcohol 13.0% by Volume

A medium-bodied, well structured classic wine. It has good varietal character in the nose and finishes with rich berry-like fruit on the palate. The oak is balanced rather than intrusive.

Excellent with veal, chicken, beef and lamb dishes.

Vintage 1870
Yountville, California
(707) 944-2788
Hours: 11:30 a.m. - 4:00 p.m.
11:30 a.m. - 8:00 p.m., Summer Weekend Hours
Credit Cards: Visa, M/C, A/X
Prices: Moderate
Reservations: Accepted
Specialties: Soup, Salad, with a strong emphasis on Chutney!

If you enjoy chutney and like to sample something that is new and different, the Vintage 1870 Chutney Kitchen is the place. Set among the oldest and most picturesque group of brick buildings in the Napa Valley, the Chutney Kitchen not only has a variety of chutney creations, but also a full menu of soups, salads, delicious sandwiches and desserts. Catering services are available for receptions, cocktail parties, lunches and dinners, or try the wine country picnics and "executive box lunches" for a special treat. Entertainment is featured on the deck during the summer season with classical guitar music. As a souvenir, take home a chutney gift pack with a full selection of chutney tastes.

Chutney Chicken Salad

3 lb. boneless whole chicken breasts
½ c. creme fraiche or heavy cream
½ c. sour cream
½ c. Hellman's mayonnaise
2 celery stalks, cut into 1'' pencil strips
½ c. shelled walnuts
½ c. apricot chutney
salt and freshly ground black pepper, to taste

Arrange chicken breasts in a single layer in a large jelly-roll pan. Spread evenly with creme fraiche and bake in a pre-heated 350° oven for 20 to 24 minutes, or until done. Remove from oven and cool. Shred meat into bite-size pieces and transfer to a bowl. Whisk sour cream and mayonnaise together in a small bowl and pour over chicken mixture. Add celery, walnuts, chutney, salt and pepper and toss well. Refrigerate, covered, for at least 4 hours. Taste and correct seasoning before serving.

Serves 4-6

Domaine
Chandon

California Drive • Yountville, California
(707) 944-8844
Hours: 11:30 a.m. - 2:30 p.m., Lunch, Every Day, May-Nov.
11:30 a.m. - 2:30 p.m., Lunch, Wed.-Sun., Nov.-May
6:00 p.m. - 9:00 p.m., Dinner, Wed.-Sat.
5:30 p.m. - 8:30 p.m., Dinner, Sunday
Closed Monday & Tuesday
Credit Cards: All Major
Prices: Moderate-Expensive
Reservations: Suggested
Specialties: French

An elegant atmosphere, delicious food uniquely prepared and the utmost attention to service makes dining at Domaine Chandon a true pleasure. The rich and warm feeling evoked here is complemented by a prix fixe menu of French delicacies, changing daily. You'll find a privacy within open spaces and have a chance to relax and enjoy any one of the Domaine Chandon's lunch or dinner entrees or the Carte du jour, offered each day by Chef Jeanty, where "the adventurous may taste innovative new ideas and featured specialties," as the menu states.

51

La Creme de Tomatoes en Croute

1 lb. yellow onion, peeled & chopped
4 T. sweet butter
3 lb. fresh tomatoes, quartered
6 cloves garlic, peeled
1 bay leaf
pinch thyme (fresh if possible)
salt and white pepper
3 c. heavy cream

Cook onions in butter until soft, then add the tomatoes and seasonings. Cook slowly, uncovered, for 3½ hours. Run through a blender or food processor and strain. Add the cream and correct the seasonings.

Croute: 1 recipe puff pastry (approximately 2 lb.)

Roll out the puff pastry to about ⅛" thick. Paint the surface with an egg wash (1 egg beaten with 1 T. water). Cut circles of pastry about 2" larger in diameter than the soup crocks (ovenproof) in which the soup will be served. Cool the soup slightly. Place it in the crocks (with a few thinly cut, julienned carrots and onion rings and leeks for garnish). Lay the circle of puff pastry on top of the crock and stretch it tight (as for a drum head) and down the sides. The egg wash side should be down, so the wash helps form a seal between the sides of the bowl and pastry. Refrigerate the crocks for 1 hour to set the pastry (can be held in the refrigerator for a day or two if the pastry is covered to prevent drying out).

La Creme de Tomatoes en Croute (Cont.)

Put egg wash on the top side of the pastry and bake for 15 minutes (or until light brown) in a 450° oven. Do not open the oven during baking, as this will cause the pastry to fall. Serve immediately in the crocks crowned with puffed pastry.

Tip: If the tomatoes are not very ripe, you can add 1 T. of tomato paste.

Le Thon Grille aux Herbs du Jardin et Pates aux Deux Citrons

(Grilled Tuna with Fresh Herbs and Lemon-Lime Pasta)

Cut tuna in ½" steaks. Marinate fresh tuna (preferably yellowfin tuna from Hawaii) in olive oil and chopped fresh herbs (lemon, thyme, oregano, basil) overnight. Before cooking, drain off excess oil. Salt and pepper steaks and lay down on pre-heated grill. Cook each side for about 3 minutes, or until medium-rare. Place on plate and rub the tuna with a small piece of sweet butter (this will help keep tuna from drying while you prepare pasta).

Les Pates Fraiches aux Deux Citrons

(Lemon and Lime pasta)

1 c. champagne
2 shallots, chopped
½ lb. sweet butter
salt
juice and zest from one lemon
juice and zest from one lime

1 lb. fresh linguini or "angel hair" pasta

Make the beurre blanc* by reducing the champagne and shallots by one half. On low heat, add the butter, piece by piece, stirring constantly. Salt to taste. Add the lemon and lime zests and some of the juice to taste. Set sauce aside and keep warm. Cook the fresh pasta in salted water for about three minutes or until "al dente." Drain off the pasta and mix it with the warm beurre blanc and citrus mixture. Correct the seasoning by adding salt and/or lemon or lime juice, if necessary.

Serves 6

* See Glossary

Ceviche
(Citric Juice-Cured Seafood)

2 lb. scallops, trimmed and cleaned
  (may use salmon, cut to size of scallops)
½ c. each: lemon, lime and orange juice
½ bundle fresh cilantro

Garnish:
1 cucumber, sliced
very thin slices of red onion
avocado slices
chopped chives

Dressing:
2 T. golden caviar
1 c. olive oil
½ c. sour cream
½ c. champagne

Marinate scallops in juices and cilantro. Mix together and let stand for 3-4 hours in the refrigerator or at room temperature. Line custard cup with thin slices of cucumbers. Drain scallops, place in custard cups and unmold on plate. Form ring on plate with onions. Place 3 slices of avocado between onions. Top with chopped chives. Whisk caviar, olive oil, sour cream and champagne. Dollop between avocado slices.

Le Sabayon au Grand Marnier avec les Framboises

(Sabayon with Grand Marnier and Raspberries)

¼ bottle Moscato wine
4½ c. granulated sugar
2 whole eggs
6 egg yolks
2 T. rum
2 T. Grand Marnier
½ t. vanilla
6 oz. whipping cream
2 baskets fresh raspberries (available berries may be substituted)
6 slices of peeled orange
candied orange peel (recipe follows)
6 mint tips

Reduce the wine by half. In a mixing bowl, blend the wine, sugar, eggs and egg yolks together and cook in a double boiler until it forms a ribbon. Cool over ice, stirring continuously with a wire whip. Add the rum, Grand Marnier and vanilla to the cool mixture (adjust to taste if desired), and fold in the whipping cream. On a dessert plate, form a ring of raspberries and pour the sabayon inside it. Place an orange slice in the center of the sabayon. Sprinkle powdered sugar through a sieve, on top. Garnish with candied orange peel and mint and put the plate in the oven briefly to glaze.

Serves 6

Candied Orange Peel

zest from one orange
grenadine syrup
Grand Marnier (if desired)

Remove the zest of an orange and cut it into julienne strips. Boil it for three minutes. Change the water and boil again for three minutes (do this through three changes of water) to remove any bitterness. Then cook the julienned zest in grenadine syrup *very* slowly (30-45 minutes) until it becomes transparent; strain. If additional flavor is desired, add a little Grand Marnier to the grenadine syrup.

NET CONTENTS
750 ML (25.4 FL OZ)

ALCOHOL 12%
BY VOLUME

CHANDON

Blanc de Noirs

NAPA VALLEY SPARKLING WINE
METHODE CHAMPENOISE
PRODUCED AND BOTTLED BY DOMAINE CHANDON, YOUNTVILLE, CA.

This flavorful, sparkling wine has a pale blush from the dark skins
of the Pinot Noir grapes.

An excellent choice to accompany many foods, particularly pates,
duck, eggs, turkey, fish and even composed salads or desserts.
It makes an entrancing display in a tall, slim flute or tulip, with
sunlight playing on its long-lasting stream of minute bubbles.
It stands up well to most meat dishes, unless they are highly spiced.
Stay away from Tex-Mex, but curry is fine.

INNER GARDEN CAFE

823 Main Street • Napa, California
(707) 224-9000
Hours: 7:30 a.m. - 5:00 p.m., Breakfast & Lunch, Mon., Tues., Wed.
7:30 a.m. - 9:00 p.m., Thursday & Friday
Credit Cards: None
Prices: Inexpensive-Moderate
Reservations: Suggested for 5 or more
Specialties: California Cuisine

Wonderful, gourmet fresh food like salads, soups and sandwiches are found at Inner Garden in Napa for breakfast and lunch. The quiches, croissant sandwiches and garden salads are made from scratch, using the most healthy and freshest ingredients around. Homemade soups are served with baguette and butter, or try any of Inner Garden's combinations of soup and salads or half-sandwiches. Fresh flowers at each table, French lace curtains and the smell of fresh herbs wafts through the air. Local artists display their works each month, with new and interesting creations all the time.

Hungarian Mushroom Soup

2 c. onion, chopped
4 T. butter
1 lb. mushrooms, sliced
2 T. fresh dill weed, chopped (or 2 t. dry dill)
2 c. stock or water
1 T. soy sauce
1 T. Hungarian paprika
3 T. flour
1 c. milk
1 t. salt
dash of pepper
2 t. fresh lemon juice
¾ c. sour cream
¼ c. fresh parsley, chopped

Saute onions in 2 T. butter for 5-10 minutes. Add mushrooms, 1 t. dill, ½ c. stock or water, soy sauce and paprika. Cover and simmer for 15 minutes. Melt remaining 2 T. butter in separate, large sauce pan. Whisk in flour, cook a few minutes, whisking constantly. Add milk. Cook, stirring frequently, over low heat until thick (about 10 minutes). Stir in mushroom mixture and remaining stock. Cover and simmer for 10-15 minutes. Before serving, add salt, pepper, lemon juice, sour cream and extra dill. Garnish with parsley.

Serves 4

Spicy Peanut Sauce

1 c. peanut butter
¼ c. sesame oil
½ c. safflower oil
½ c. soy sauce
½ c. sherry
½ c. brown sugar
1 c. water or stock
¼ c. lemon juice
¼ c. Hoisin sauce *
½ c. catsup
1 t. cayenne
1 t. Chinese five-spice *
2 cloves garlic, minced

Combine all ingredients in saucepan or skillet. Cook over low heat, stirring constantly with whisk until thick and smooth (10-15 minutes). If sauce is too thick, add water. Spoon over shredded lettuce, shredded chicken, cilantro and water chestnuts. Sauce is also good over cooked rice and vegetables.

* Available in Chinese grocery stores

Indonesian Rice Salad

2 c. cooked rice, cooled
½ c. raisins
2-3 scallions, chopped
¼ c. sesame seeds
½ c. water chestnuts, sliced
¼ c. cashews
1 bell pepper (red or green), chopped
1 celery stalk, sliced
½ c. parsley, chopped
½ c. snow peas, sliced on diagonal

Combine all ingredients and toss with Ginger-Lemon Dressing to coat (recipe follows).

Serves 6-8

Ginger-Lemon Dressing

1½ c. fresh orange juice
1 c. safflower oil
½ c. soy sauce
¼ c. dry sherry
½ c. lemon juice
4 garlic cloves, minced
1 T. ginger root, grated
salt and pepper to taste

Combine all ingredients in glass jar and shake well until completely mixed. Pour over rice salad until well-coated.

JOHN ASH & CO.

RESTAURANT AND WINE SHOP

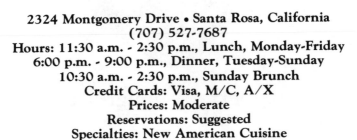

2324 Montgomery Drive • Santa Rosa, California
(707) 527-7687
Hours: 11:30 a.m. - 2:30 p.m., Lunch, Monday-Friday
6:00 p.m. - 9:00 p.m., Dinner, Tuesday-Sunday
10:30 a.m. - 2:30 p.m., Sunday Brunch
Credit Cards: Visa, M/C, A/X
Prices: Moderate
Reservations: Suggested
Specialties: New American Cuisine

For American Cuisine in a country French atmosphere, try John Ash and Co., located in Santa Rosa. Many premium wines are poured by the glass here, and they also have an extensive local wine list. The daily specials are something new to try, or you can order off John Ash's interesting and delicious menu, featuring entrees like stuffed quail, Sonoma rack of lamb and a selection of fresh fish. Everything is prepared to perfection and served beautifully with a nouvelle French look.

63

Raspberry Vinaigrette

2 eggs
⅓ to ½ c. good raspberry vinegar
½ t. finely minced shallot
3 T. raspberry juice or fresh raspberries (seeded)
1 to 1½ c. good oil (½ peanut/½ light olive)
salt and white pepper
heavy cream

In processor or by hand, beat eggs, vinegar, shallot and raspberry juice together until well blended. Slowly beat in oil to make the emulsion. Correct seasoning; thin, if necessary, with cream. Store refrigerated. Use as dressing for salads. Especially good on endive or on scallops which have been marinated an hour or two in straight raspberry vinegar.

Choux Pastry

½ c. butter (1 stick)
1 c. water
1 c. flour
½ t. salt or 1 t. sugar
4 large eggs

Heat butter and water until butter is melted and mixture is bubbling. Take off heat and quickly beat in flour until mixture forms a smooth paste. Beat in salt or sugar. Beat in eggs, one at a time, until thoroughly incorporated. With spoon or pastry bag, place on baking sheet; glaze with egg wash*. Bake at 400°.

"Choux au fromage" Appetizer

Beat ½ c. grated gruyere, asiago or other full-flavored cheese into; mixture above along with the eggs. Form into small puffs; glaze and top with sesame or poppy seeds. Serve warm from the oven or cool and fill with a flavored cream cheese mixture.

* See Glossary

"Profiteroles d'oeufs poches a la puree de haricots verts" Entree

(Poached Eggs & Green Bean Puree Puffs)

Make large puffs, either plain or cheese (previous recipe).

Green Bean Puree:
Cook one pound tender green beans in boiling, salted water 5 minutes or until just tender. Drain and puree in a processor. Reserve a few whole beans for garnish.

Tomato Sauce:

8 tomatoes, peeled and seeded
½ t. salt
branch of thyme (½ t. dry)
vinegar to taste
olive oil to taste
2 T. butter (to finish)

In small saucepan, simmer tomatoes, salt and thyme for 15 minutes. Add vinegar, oil and puree. Reheat and beat in butter just before serving. About 20 minutes before serving, reheat choux puffs in moderate oven. Heat 1 T. butter until nut brown. Add green bean puree and heat through; correct seasoning. Spoon puree into puff, top with poached egg and julienne of whole reserved beans. Replace hat and spoon tomato sauce around.

My Grandmother's Chicken

¼ lb. bacon
1 T. oil
2 cut-up chickens
2 onions, thinly sliced
3 garlic cloves, minced
4 carrots, diced
½ bunch of celery, cut in diagonal slices
3 T. butter
2 c. chicken stock
3 T. tomato paste
3 c. fruity red wine
2 t. fresh thyme
3 bay leaves
1 T. orange rind
6-8 juniper berries
blanched vegetables
sauteed mushrooms
dried tomatoes

In a large saute pan, cook bacon until crisp. Remove and reserve bacon. Add oil to the drippings and brown the chicken until brown all over. If desired, season lightly with salt and pepper. Remove and reserve chicken. Add onions to the pan with garlic, carrots, celery and butter. Saute until vegetables are soft but not brown. Add reserved chicken and bacon, chicken stock, tomato paste, wine, thyme, bay leaves, orange rind and juniper berries. Bring the mixture to a boil; reduce to a simmer and cover. Place in a pre-heated 350° oven and bake for 45 minutes. Remove from

My Grandmother's Chicken (Cont.)

oven; pick out chicken pieces and set aside. Strain sauce into a clean saucepan and reduce for about 15 minutes, or to desired consistency. Correct seasonings. Return chicken to sauce. Garnish with freshly blanched vegetables, mushrooms and dried tomatoes. Add them to the dish just in time to heat through before serving.

Serves 6-8

Scallops of Fresh Salmon with Mustard Cream and Mushrooms

6½ oz. very fresh salmon, sliced very thin (as for smoked salmon)
4 large white mushroom caps, well washed
juice of ½ lemon
salt and pepper
sprigs of fresh parsley or chervil

Sauce Ingredients:
4 T. heavy cream
1 egg yolk
juice of ½ lemon
1 t. Dijon mustard
salt and pepper
5 T. olive oil
1 t. Meaux mustard (with grains)
whipped cream (if necessary)

In bowl or mixer, whip heavy cream until it becomes thick but not stiff; keep cold. In another bowl, mix egg yolk with lemon juice, Dijon mustard, pinch of salt and pepper. Beat vigorously while gradually adding oil; continue beating until sauce becomes firm. Add Meaux mustard and whipped cream. If necessary, adjust seasoning with salt and pepper. On 4 very cold plates, arrange slices of salmon (raw), well spread out. Sprinkle with salt and pepper and cover with sauce. Dice mushrooms caps and toss with lemon juice, salt and pepper. Arrange diced mushrooms like a bouquet on each plate and garnish with sprigs of parsley or

Scallops of Fresh Salmon with Mustard Cream and Mushrooms (Cont.)

chervil. The sauce quantity is for 8 servings because it is difficult to make less. To serve 4 people, the extra sauce may be refrigerated and used to season a green salad or cold cooked fish. After sauce has been in refrigerator, rewhip to make it supple.

Serves 4

Oysters and Mussels

fresh mussels and/or clams

Mussels Marinere:
4 c. white wine
1 c. minced green onions
½ t. minced garlic
½ c. glace de poisson (reduced fish stock)
½ t. each: thyme, oregano, basil, pepper
12 T. butter
⅓ c. chopped parsley
heavy cream

Simmer all marinere ingredients (except cream) together for 10-15 minutes. For each person, use ¾ to 1 c. of mixture along with fresh mussels and/or clams and simmer in covered pot until shellfish open. Remove fish; reduce liquid by ⅓. Add a splash of heavy cream and pour over fish in a bowl.

Tenderloin of Pork with Raspberry Vinegar

2 lb. pork tenderloin (not loin)

Marinade:
¼ c. olive oil
½ t. whole thyme
¼ t. whole sage
¼ t. salt
a couple grindings of black pepper

flour for dusting
2 T. clarified butter*
salt and pepper to taste
clarified butter
½ c. mushrooms
1 t. minced shallot
1½ c. good beef, pork or veal stock
2 t. raspberry vinegar
2 T. sweetened raspberry puree
    (can be made from frozen and strained to remove seeds)
1 T. soy sauce
1 T. brandy

Trim whole tenderloins of any fat and silverskin. Marinate pork for at least 2 hours or overnight. Remove pork from marinade, lightly dust with flour and saute in clarified butter, turning frequently until lightly brown all over (approximately 5 minutes).

Tenderloin of Pork

with Raspberry Vinegar (Cont.)

Season with salt and pepper. Remove pork to warm platter
(NOTE: pork should be lightly pink inside; DO NOT
OVERCOOK). Degrease saute pan and add a bit more clarified
butter, mushrooms and shallots and saute until shallots are soft,
not brown. Add stock, vinegar, raspberry puree, soy sauce,
brandy and reduce by ⅓ until sauce is desired consistency. Place
ribbon of sauce on plate. Slice tenderloin on the bias and arrange
attractively over sauce. Garnish with orange zest and fresh
raspberries.

* See Glossary   *Serves 4*

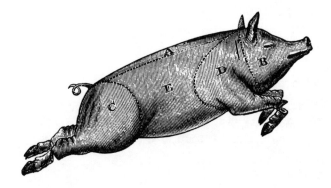

Choux au Chocolate

Make sweetened choux puffs, omitting salt (see recipe elsewhere in this section). Fill with creme Chantilly (flavored whipped cream) or pastry cream. Top with hot chocolate walnut sauce (recipe below). Garnish with a drop of raspberry sauce or fresh strawberries.

Chocolate Walnut Sauce

½ c. half & half
1 c. sugar
4 oz. bittersweet chocolate
¼ lb. butter
2 whipped egg yolks
1 t. vanilla
¼ lb. butter
¾ c. chopped walnuts

Heat half & half and sugar until sugar is dissolved. Add chocolate and butter and stir until melted. Remove from heat and stir in egg yolks, vanilla, butter and walnuts. Store leftovers in refrigerator and reheat over double boiler as needed.

Makes 3 cups

California Nut Torte

Crust:
1⅓ c. ground almonds
3½ T. pastry flour
2½ T. sugar
⅓ c. sweet butter, cut into bits

Filling:
1 c. + 2½ T. brown sugar
2 eggs
1 egg yolk
½ t. baking powder
1¾ c. coarsely chopped walnuts and filberts (mixed)
1 c. coconut, shredded
½ c. flour

Mix the crust ingredients with paddle in mixing bowl until just incorporated and still slightly crumbly. Press into 8" x 8" x ½" cake pan, going ⅓ up the side of the pan. Blend first 4 filling ingredients in mixer with paddle. Add remaining ingredients. Pour filling into prepared crust. Bake 25 minutes at 350°. It should be very soft and "caramelly" in center. Dust with powdered sugar and serve with creme anglaise*.

Makes one 8-inch round cake

* See Glossary

Chocolate-Apricot Torte

Crust:
3 oz. unsweetened chocolate, chopped roughly
2 c. nuts, chopped roughly
1½ c. flour
¾ c. brown sugar
½ t. salt
½ c. cold butter, cut up into small pieces
2 T. cold water
2 t. vanilla

Filling:
11 oz. dried apricots, chopped
¾-1 c. sugar
¾ c. water
3 T. flour
juice of ½ a lemon
¼ c. Grand Marnier

Mix first 5 crust ingredients together. Cut in butter until crumbly. Add water and vanilla and mix until just moistened-- not to a doughy consistency. Grease an 8 or 9-inch springform pan and pat ⅓ of dough into bottom and up 1" along the sides. Set aside. Combine first 5 filling ingredients and bring slowly to a boil over low heat (in a saucepan). Reduce heat and simmer for about 25 minutes. Remove from heat and cool. Add Grand Marnier to flavor and to your taste (about ¼ plus cup). Chop or puree mixture if big pieces of apricot remain after cooking. Place

Chocolate-Apricot Torte (Cont.)

filling into lined springform pan and spread mixture with a spatula to even out. Crumble remaining dough (¹/₃) over top. Sprinkle with some Grand Marnier. Bake at 350° for 40-45 minutes. Cool and remove from pan. Sprinkle with additional Grand Marnier.

Makes 1 8 or 9-inch springform pan

California
CHARDONNAY

PRODUCED AND BOTTLED BY

NAPA, CALIFORNIA • 375 ML
ALCOHOL 13.3% BY VOLUME

Well balanced, lush, tropical fruit flavor and aroma; lingering aftertaste.

Goes well with rich, flavorful foods.

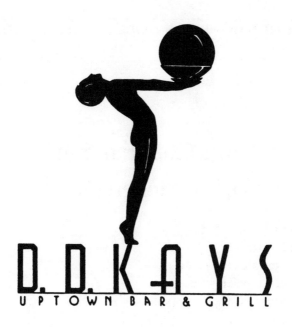

811 Coombs • Napa, California
(707) 224-5925
Hours: 11:30 a.m. - 2:30 p.m., Lunch, Tuesday-Friday
5:30 p.m. - 10:00 p.m., Dinner, Tuesday-Sunday
10:30 a.m. - 2:30 p.m., Sunday Brunch
Closed Monday
Credit Cards: Visa, M/C
Prices: Moderate
Reservations: Suggested
Specialties: Regional Eclectic Fresh Food

Using the freshest ingredients offered by local markets and paying keen attention to every detail are the specialties at D.D. Kays, located in Napa. A varied menu with daily specials, a full range of appetizers, entrees and desserts, as well as a large selection of Napa Valley wines is available. You'll enjoy the art deco motif throughout D.D. Kays, with ceiling fans, colors of pink and black and fresh gladiolas in black, sculptured vases. The music also carries out the theme with the sounds of old favorites like the Andrew Sisters. The service is excellent and each meal is presented with innovation and style.

Chili Cheddar Soup
with Chicken Broth

10 oz. sweet butter *
8 oz. bread flour
1 gal. chicken stock boiled
2½ oz. canned green chilies
1 large yellow onion, chopped
2 T. garlic, minced
2 T. shallots, minced
1 c. sherry wine
12 oz. grated cheddar cheese
salt and white pepper to taste

In a six-quart saucepan, melt the butter and the flour together, forming a roux**. Cook for five minutes, stirring. Bring chicken stock to a boil. Add stock to the roux a little at a time, forming a sauce. After adding all the stock, simmer 30 minutes. Meanwhile, saute the chopped chilies, onion, garlic and shallot until soft and add it to the stock. Then add the wine and cheddar cheese, mixing well. Season to taste with salt and pepper. (Egg yolks and cream may be used to thicken the soup.)

Serves 4-6

* Reserve a little butter to saute chilies, onions, garlic and shallots.

** See Glossary

Radicchio & Arrugula Salad with Raspberry Vinaigrette and Bucheron on Crouton

4 heads of radicchio
6 bunches arrugula
6-10 oz. Bucheron cheese
25 croutons

Raspberry Vinaigrette:
½ c. raspberry vinegar
½ c. creme fraiche *
1 t. each salt and pepper
3 t. fresh assorted herbs
   (tarragon, basil, rosemary, sage, etc.)
¼ c.white wine
1 c. olive oil

Combine all the ingredients for the vinaigrette, except the oil. Mix well and gradually whisk in oil; set aside. On chilled plates, remove the outer leaves of the radicchio and line the plates with the leaves. After you have washed the arrugula, put one bunch at a time in a bowl and toss gently with about 2 oz. of the raspberry vinaigrette. While you are tossing the arrugula, heat the bucheron in a moderate to high oven (400-450°). Place dressed arrugula on a plate with radicchio. After the bucheron has been heated through (about 3-5 minutes), spread on croutons (4 to a salad).

Serves 4-6

* See Glossary

Pasta Alfredo with Fettucini

3 lb. fresh fettucini
¼ c. sweet butter
1 c. chopped walnuts
1 c. dry white wine
¾ c. butter
1 qt. heavy cream
2 T. fresh or frozen pesto
1 t. salt
4 cloves garlic, minced
freshly ground black pepper, to taste
2 c. fresh-grated parmesan cheese

In a gallon of boiling, salted, oiled water, cook the fettucini until al dente. Place in ice water to prevent further cooking; reserve. In a large saute pan, add butter. Saute walnuts, until brown. Add white wine and butter. Reduce slightly, then add cream, pesto, salt and garlic; mix well. Add the black pepper to taste. Add the cheese; mix well. Reheat the pasta and fold into the sauce. More cream may be needed, as fresh pasta will absorb moisture.

Serves 4-6

Chicken Duexelle

8 oz. mushrooms, chopped fine
1 small white onion
2 t. shallots, chopped
1 c. chopped chicken livers
1 oz. olive oil
1 oz. clarified butter **
2 oz. dry white wine
½ c. heavy whipping cream
4 oz. parmesan cheese
six 6-8-oz. boned chicken breasts
salt
pepper
flour for dusting the breasts
6 oz. white wine
2 c. chicken stock

Chop the mushrooms, onions, shallots and chicken livers. In a large saute pan, add the oil and clarified butter and heat until hot. Saute the onion, mushrooms, shallots and chicken livers until soft. Add 2 oz. white wine and the cream. Cook slowly until reduced. Add the parmesan cheese. Fold in and cool. Season the chicken breasts with salt and pepper to taste. Slice the breasts inward about 2", under the tenderloin. Stuff with duexelle* (mushroom mixture), folding the tenderloin over. Dust lightly with flour and place the stuffed side down in a greased baking dish. Place in a 500° pre-heated oven. Flip the breasts after 7 minutes; return to oven for 7 more minutes. Add the remaining

Chicken Duexelle (Cont.)

wine and chicken stock. Place back in oven for 3 minutes. Place the breasts on serving plates. Reduce the stock on the stove. Spoon sauce over each breast.

Serves 4-6

* Duexelle stuffing mix may be prepared in advance.

** See Glossary

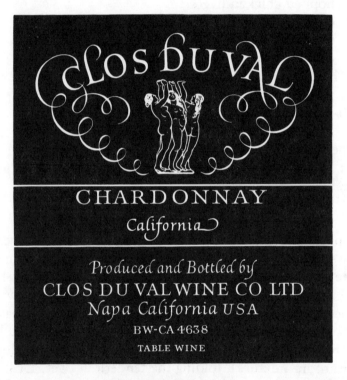

Complex components blend beautifully with richness and elegance. Medium body; rich, lush apple, lemon flavors; crisp, rich texture and long, full finish.

Delicious with Shellfish and delicate seafood, fowl dishes and cream pastas.

82

Bread Pudding

4 eggs
1½ c. granulated sugar
2 t. cinnamon
2 t. nutmeg
1 loaf of stale French bread, cut into 1" cubes
2 c. cream
2 c. milk
1 c. raisins
1 c. walnuts

Bourbon Sauce:
1¼ sticks of sweet butter
1 c. sifted confectioners sugar
1 egg
4-6 T. bourbon

Pre-heat oven to 350°. Grease a 9x13x2" baking dish. In a bowl, beat the eggs; add the sugar, cinnamon and nutmeg. Place cubed bread in baking dish. Pour egg mixture over the bread. Alternately pour cream and milk over bread. Gently stir in raisins and walnuts. Place pan in shallow water bath* (about ⅛"). Cook for 1 hour or until milk and eggs are absorbed completely into the bread. *Bourbon Sauce:* Melt butter; take off heat and gradually add sifted sugar. Beat in egg; add bourbon. To serve, place 1 oz. of Bourbon Sauce on bottom of plate. Place portioned piece of bread pudding on top of sauce and place another ounce of sauce on top. Put in high oven (500°) for 5-7 minutes.

Serves 4-6

* See Glossary

THE

CHRISTIAN BROTHERS

VINTNERS SINCE 1882

NAPA VALLEY
CHARDONNAY

PRODUCED AND BOTTLED BY
THE CHRISTIAN BROTHERS, ST. HELENA, CALIFORNIA
750ML • ALCOHOL 13% BY VOLUME • BW 4497 • PRODUCT OF USA

A deep brilliant yellow wine with strong Chardonnay varietal character, the vanilla-like bouquet of French oak, crisp acid, and a lingering, velvety finish.

Pairs well with fresh Salmon with Summer Vegetables and Cucumber Salad Poached Chicken Breast with Cream Tarragon Sauce.

208 Wilson at Railroad Square • Santa Rosa, California
(707) 528-4355
Hours: 5:30 p.m. - 10:00 p.m., Dinner, Tuesday-Thursday
5:00 p.m. - 10:00 p.m., Dinner, Friday & Saturday
5:00 p.m. - 9:00 p.m., Dinner, Sunday
Closed Monday
Credit Cards: All Major
Prices: Moderate
Reservations: Suggested
Specialties: French

    Set in the historic Railroad Square in old-town Santa Rosa, La Gare features an array of delectable French dishes for dinner every evening but Monday. This small and intimate restaurant has a varied menu with fine hors d'oeuvres, soup of the day and consomme. Entrees include Prawns Provencale, Chateaubriand, veal and beef dishes with a vegetarian special as well. The desserts are delicious and La Gare features imported French wines, as well as local Napa and Sonoma varietals.

85

Duck Pate'

1 whole fresh Petaluma duck, approx. 4 lb.
2 onions, chopped
3 garlic cloves, crushed
4 oz. salted butter (1 cube)
1 lb. duck livers (use chicken livers if duck is not available)
8 oz. lean pork
3 oz. heavy cream
3 oz. Cabernet Sauvignon
3 oz. brandy
2 lb. bacon or pork fat
8 oz. fresh spinach

Skin duck. Take breast off and put to one side for later use. Take rest of meat off the carcass. Saute onions and garlic in butter until soft. Add chicken or duck livers, lean pork, duck meat (not breast). Add cream, brandy and wine; mix well and cook on top of stove for 40 minutes. Remove from stove and liquidise (mince finely). Take pate tin and line with bacon, leaving enough bacon hanging over tin to cover pate. Place minced pate in tin, covering ⅓. Put a layer of spinach over mix. Slice duck breast and arrange over spinach. Top with more pate mixture. Cover with overhanging bacon. To a roasting tin, add water ⅓ full to make a Bain Marie*. Place pate tin and bacon on top and cook in oven for 1½ hours at 350°. Cool, turn out and serve.

Makes 2 pates

* See "Water Bath" in Glossary

Prawns Bordelaise

8 prawns (under 15 to the lb. or 1-1¼ oz. each)
flour
1 egg (for egg wash)
2 T. oil
salt and pepper
¼ t. shallots
¼ t. garlic
2 oz. butter
¼ t. lemon juice
1 t. parsley
 c. white wine

Devein shrimp and butterfly through the back. Dust with flour
and dip in egg wash*. Heat a skillet with approximately 2 T. oil.
When hot (not smoking), lay prawns flat and brown them. Turn
prawns and add salt and pepper. Drain oil, add shallots, garlic,
butter and lemon juice. Saute quickly, then add parsley and white
wine and let sauce thicken. If sauce breaks, add a little more white
wine to bring it back to proper consistency.

Serves 2

* See Glossary

Tournedos de Boeuf a l'estragon

salt and pepper
2 6-oz. tournedos (filet of beef)
1 T. oil
¼ t. fresh tarragon
¼ t. shallots
¼ c. red wine
demi glace (see glossary)
1 t. butter
¼ t. chopped parsley

Salt and pepper tournedos. Heat oil in a pan (searing hot). Sear
each side and roast/broil to proper doneness. Drain oil, remove
tournedos. Add tarragon, shallots and red wine. Let reduce until
almost dry, then add demi glace. Finish with a dab of butter and
sprinkle with chopped parsley to garnish.

Serves 2

Riz de Veau Financiere

10 oz. veal sweetbreads
mire poix (carrots, celery, leek, parsley, bay leaf, thyme, onion,
   black pepper) *
2 oz. chicken stock
2 T. oil
salt
pepper
¼ c. mushrooms
2 T. onions, diced
2 T. black olives
½ c. Madeira wine
2 c. heavy whipping cream
¼ t. parsley, chopped

Blanch* sweetbreads in boiling water for 1 minute. Leave in cold water to remove blood; press under a board to remove excess water and then remove sinew. Braise in oven with mire poix and chicken stock at 350° for 45 minutes; let cool. Cut into cubes. In hot oil, saute quickly and add salt and pepper, mushrooms, onions and olives. Deglace* with Madeira wine. Reduce, then add heavy whipping cream. When thick enough, serve and garnish with parsley.

* See Glossary

Serves 2

A medium-straw color is apparent in each glass of Glen Ellen's Chardonnay.
Its aromas are reminiscent of Bosc pears with hints of apricot. The flavors
are a classic varietal definition of Chardonnay...pear and apple-like, layered
with accents of cinnamon, spice and oak.

This is a most versatile Chardonnay. It easily makes the transition from a
before meal drink to its place at the dinner table. Seafood and poultry
dishes, especially those prepared on the outdoor grill, create an ideal
pairing.

90

La Province

525 College Avenue • Santa Rosa, California
(707) 526-6233
Lunch, Tue. - Fri.
Dinner, Mon. - Sat.
Credit Cards: Visa, M/C, A/X
Prices: Moderate
Reservations: Recommended
Specialties: French Continental featuring Veal, Chicken & Seafood

French continental dining is the specialty at La Province, located in Santa Rosa. Cheg Josef Keller prepares his outstanding gourmet sauces of garlic herb, lemon dill and milled curry to complement any of the menu selections which feature veal, seafood and chicken dishes. Private dining in one of La Province's elegant dining rooms is offered to those who want to relax and taste a delicious meal. Seating for 6 to 50 people is available.

91

Chicken or Veal Marsala

4 chicken breast halves, boned and skinned, *or*
12 ounces veal, thinly sliced
salt and pepper or seasoning salt (to taste)
flour
2 oz. butter
2 oz. peanut or vegetable oil
2 T. parsley, chopped
½ medium onion, chopped
Worchestershire Sauce (to taste)
¼ c. dry Marsala wine
2 c. brown sauce *
1 c. sliced mushrooms

Season meat with salt and pepper and dredge in flour. Saute meat in butter and oil until lightly browned. Add parsley, onion, Worchestershire Sauce and Marsala wine to pan and bring to a boil. Add brown sauce and return to a boil; lower heat and simmer, covered, for 10 minutes. Remove lid, add mushrooms and simmer uncovered an additional 5 minutes. Serve with rice or noodles.

Serves 2

* Available in the Gourmet section of your grocery store or in a Gourmet Specialty Shop or see Glossary.

Beef Bourguignone

2 lbs. top round, cubed
2 T. oil
2 T. flour
2 c. red wine
6 c. beef stock
¼ lb. bacon
1½ doz. pearl onions
½ c. chopped parsley
3 medium tomatoes, chunked
¼ lb. mushrooms
croutons

Roast chunks of beef in hot oil until light brown. Dust with flour.
Add wine and stock to beef; bring to a boil. Simmer approximately
1½ hours. Saute bacon until light brown. Add pearl onions, parsley,
tomatoes, and mushrooms. Bring to a quick simmer. Remove
from heat and keep for garnish. When ready to serve, top beef
with garnish and sprinkle with croutons.

Serves 6

Red Snapper Tarragon

2 lbs. red snapper
½ onion
3 c. fish stock
⅛ lb. butter
2 T. flour
½ pint half and half
½ c. heavy cream
¼ bunch fresh tarragon (or 1 t. dried)
lemon juice
soy sauce
seasoning salt

Poach fish and onion in fish stock until half done. Remove fish from liquid and set aside. Make a roux* with butter and flour. Stir into simmering fish stock and simmer for ½ hour; strain. Add cream, half and half, and tarragon and finish seasoning with lemon juice, soy sauce, and seasoning salt. Befor serving, heat up the fish in the sauce until cooked through.

Serves 4

* See Glossary

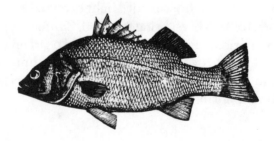

Le Rhone

1234 Main Street • St. Helena, California
(707) 963-0240
Hours: 6:00 p.m. - 10:00 p.m., Wednesday-Sunday
Closed Monday and Tuesday
Credit Cards: None
Prices: Expensive
Reservations: Required
Specialties: French

Fine French cuisine, served a la carte or prix fixe, is featured at Le Rhone, located in St. Helena. This small and authentic French restaurant has been given the prestigious Golden Fork Award, as well as being honored by the California Restaurant Writers Association. It is open for dinner only, with a changing menu each evening of hors d'oeuvres, entrees and desserts. A number of choices are available from both menus.

La Daube a la Cote du Rhone Red

½ lb. bacon (cut in thin slices)
3 lb. sirloin beef
2 carrots, sliced
1 onion, sliced
2 T. brandy
½ c. red Cote du Rhone
1 T. tomato sauce
½ c. butter

In a large sauce pan, saute bacon, beef, carrots and onions until the beef looses its pinkness. Remove the excess fat and flame with brandy. Add wine and tomato sauce. Simmer for 1 hour covered. Remove the beef to a warm plate and add butter to the sauce. Pour the sauce over the beef and serve with potatoes or pasta.

Gateau Normand Apple Cake

prepared puff pastry
2 c. apple sauce
Glace Royale (recipe follows)
1 c. chopped almonds

Roll out the puff pastry ⅛" to ¼" thick and place half of it in a shallow oblong baking dish. Spread a ¾" thick layer of very thick apple sauce over pastry. Cover apple sauce with the other half of pastry and seal the edges together. Spread a thin layer of Glace Royale on top (recipe follows) and sprinkle with chopped almonds. Bake in pre-heated 400° oven for 30 minutes or until the top is crusty and starting to brown. Serve in slices.

Glace Royale

1 c. powdered sugar
1 egg white

Blend sugar and egg white together.

CLOS DU BOIS

PROPRIETOR'S RESERVE

100%
Cabernet Sauvignon

ALEXANDER VALLEY

MADE & BOTTLED BY CLOS DU BOIS WINERY
HEALDSBURG, CALIFORNIA USA • ALCOHOL 13% BY VOL.

A smooth, medium-bodied wine, beautifully balanced with rich, forward flavors of berries and herbs.

An excellent accompaniment to many meats, including beef, lamb, duck and wild game.

Madrona Manor

1001 Westside Road • Healdsburg, California
(707) 433-4231
Hours: 6:00 p.m. - 9:00 p.m., Dinner
10:30 a.m. - 1:30 p.m., Sunday Brunch
Credit Cards: Visa, M/C, A/X
Prices: Expensive
Reservations: Suggested & Appreciated
Specialties: Modified California Cuisine

Picturesquely set right in the heart of California wine country is Madrona Manor, a beautiful three-story mansion built in 1880. Two dining rooms with majestic, vaulted ceilings and fantastic views of the dry creek valley of Sonoma County await you for a truly unique and memorable dining experience. The prix fixe menu changes daily, and a la carte items are also available. Fresh seafood and produce are always on the menu, with a large variety of other delectable items as well. The kitchen at Madrona Manor utilizes a brick oven, smokehouse and herb garden to prepare outstanding and creative dinners and Sunday brunch. You'll also enjoy simply browsing through the mansion itself, with its hand-carved woodwork, high ceilings, many original furnishings and bay windows.

99

Bran Muffins

1 c. bran
1 c. boiling water
½ c. melted shortening
2 beaten eggs
1½ c. sugar
1½ t. baking soda
1 t. salt
2 c. buttermilk
2½ c. flour
2 c. dry bran

Mix first 3 ingredients. In a large bowl, mix the remaining ingredients, except the 2 cups of dry bran. Combine with the shortening mixture. Add the 2 cups of dry bran and stir well. Cover and store in refrigerator at least overnight. Bake in muffin tins at 400° for 20 minutes.

Yield: 3 dozen

Sour Cream Vegetable Salad

1 c. cucumber, sliced
1 c. tomato, sliced
1 c. onion, sliced
1 T. vinegar
1 T. horseradish
1 t. salt
1 c. sour cream

Combine the cucumbers, tomato and onion in a bowl. In another bowl, mix vinegar, horseradish, salt and sour cream. Mix the dressing thoroughly with the vegetables. Serve on a bed of escarole or lettuce leaves.

Serves 6

101

Garlic Mashed Potatoes

2 heads of garlic, about 30 cloves
4 T. butter
2 T. flour
1 c. boiling milk
¼ t. salt, pinch of pepper
2½ lbs. baking potatoes
4 T. softened butter
salt and pepper
3-4 T. whipping cream
4 T. minced parsley

Saute garlic with butter for about 20 minutes in a covered pan. Blend flour into butter mixture. Beat in boiling milk, add salt and pepper. Boil potatoes until tender, mash, beat in butter, a tablespoon at a time and add salt and pepper. Shortly before serving, mix the hot garlic sauce into the hot potatoes. Add the cream by spoonfuls but do not thin the puree too much. Garnish with parsley. Turn into a warm vegetable dish.

Served 6-8.

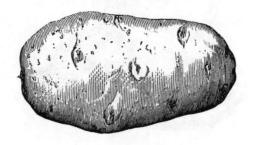

Marmalade

miniature Mandarin oranges,
   or any combination of citrus fruit
sugar
water

Process the fruit through the slicing blade of a food processor.
Place in a bowl, cover with cold water and let stand overnight.
Cook the fruit in the same water until the peels are tender.
Weigh the whole batch and add an equal weight of sugar. Cook
until the syrup gives the jelly test. Stir frequently to prevent
scorching. Pour immediately into hot, sterilized jars and seal at
once.

Soupirs de nonnes (Nun's Sighs) or Churros

1 c. water
¾ c. butter
½ t. salt
1 t. sugar
½ t. vanilla
1 c. flour
4 eggs
oil for frying

In a saucepan, mix together water, butter, salt and sugar. Add vanilla. Bring to a boil. When butter has melted completley, remove from heat and beat in flour. Return to heat and cook until the mixture rolls from the sides of the pan and there is a slight film of butter in the bottom of the pan. Add 4 eggs, one at a time, mixing well until each egg is absorbed. Heat deep fat in a pan until it is moderately hot. Place dough in pastry bag with a #6 star tip. Pipe into the preheated fat. When golden brown on both sides, drain well and serve with lots of butter and jam.

Makes about 20 3" pieces

104

Pumpkin Chiffon Pie

1 T. gelatin
¼ c. cold water
1½ c. canned or home-cooked pumpkin
1 c. brown sugar
3 egg yolks
2 t. cinnamon
½ t. ginger
¼ c. allspice
½ t. salt
3 egg whites
2 T. granulated sugar
1 T. grated orange rind
½ c. heavy cream
pastry shell, baked
whipped cream

Soften gelatin in cold water. Combine the pumpkin, brown sugar, egg yolks, spices and salt in the top of a double boiler. Cook over hot, not boiling, water until thickened, stirring constantly. Add softened gelatin to hot pumpkin mixture and stir until dissolved. Remove from hot water. Chill until mixture begins to thicken. Beat egg whites until stiff but not dry. Beat in granulated sugar. Fold into cooled pumpkin mixture. Add orange rind and heavy cream and fold into pumpkin mixture. Pour into baked shell. Garnish with whipped cream.

ROMBAUER
VINEYARDS

Napa Valley
CABERNET SAUVIGNON

PRODUCED AND BOTTLED BY ROMBAUER VINEYARDS
ST. HELENA, CALIFORNIA
ALCOHOL 12.9% BY VOLUME

This superb wine has rich blackberry and herbal flavors with smokey French oak overtones. It is rich with stylish tannins, excellently balanced with a beautiful harmony between all its flavors and components. This wine has grace, charm and finesse.

Pairs well with beef and lamb entrees as well as rich pasta dishes. It is excellent with the finest of cuisines.

BAR & GRILL

902 Main Street • Napa, California
(707) 257-7767
Hours: 11:30 a.m. - 5:30 p.m., Lunch, Monday-Saturday
From 5:30 p.m., Dinner, Every Night
Credit Cards: Visa, M/C, A/X
Prices: Moderate
Reservations: Suggested
Specialties: California-American Cuisine

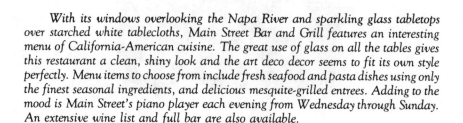

With its windows overlooking the Napa River and sparkling glass tabletops over starched white tablecloths, Main Street Bar and Grill features an interesting menu of California-American cuisine. The great use of glass on all the tables gives this restaurant a clean, shiny look and the art deco decor seems to fit its own style perfectly. Menu items to choose from include fresh seafood and pasta dishes using only the finest seasonal ingredients, and delicious mesquite-grilled entrees. Adding to the mood is Main Street's piano player each evening from Wednesday through Sunday. An extensive wine list and full bar are also available.

Fried Cheese and Zucchini

8 slices Jack cheese
½ c. (or more, if needed) Japanese bread crumbs
1 c. flour
1 qt. buttermilk
4 small zucchini

Slice cheese ¼" thick; slice zucchini. Make batter of flour and buttermilk. Dip cheese into batter and bread crumbs; repeat. Dip zucchini into batter and bread crumbs only once. Heat frying oil to 375°. Fry cheese and zucchini until golden brown.

Serves 4

Cajun-Style Linguini

18 oz. chicken breast, sliced
18 oz. Andouille sausage, sliced
1 red bell pepper, julienned
1 green bell pepper, julienned
2 oz. clarified butter *
2 t. white pepper
1 t. salt
1 t. cayenne
1 t. black pepper
1 t. dried sweet basil
½ t. dry mustard
1 bottle beer
18 oz. unsalted butter, cut in pieces
32 oz. linguini (fresh preferred)

Saute chicken breast, Andouille sausage, and red and green peppers in clarified butter. Add all seasoning and beer; simmer for 4 minutes. Remove from heat and add butter pieces; whip until dissolved. Cook fresh pasta for 90 seconds and add to sauce. Serve immediately.

Serves 6

* See Glossary

Grilled Chicken Breast
with Sun-Dried Tomato Pesto

4 oz. sun-dried tomatoes
2 oz. pine nuts
2 bunches fresh basil
2 oz. grated parmesan
½ c. olive oil
¼ c. garlic
6 whole chicken breasts

Sun-dried tomato pesto: Place the sun-dried tomatoes, pine nuts, basil, grated parmesan, olive oil and garlic into the food processor and rough chop. Grill or barbecue the chicken breast and serve with the pesto on top.

Serves 6

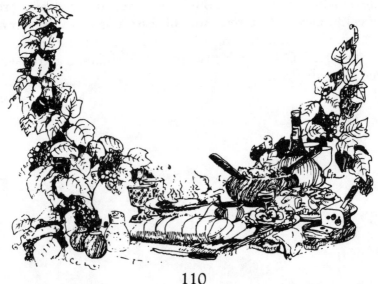

Gaspacho Sorbet with Garden Vegetables

2 large, ripe tomatoes, chopped
1 large, sweet green pepper, chopped
1 garlic clove
½ c. fresh mixed herbs (chives, parsley, basil, chervil, tarragon)
½ c. olive oil
1 T. chopped parsley
3 Sereno chilies
3 T. lemon juice
3 c. chicken stock
1 sweet yellow onion, chopped
1 c. cucumber, diced and grated
1½ t. salt
½ t. paprika
½ c. dry bread crumbs
½ t. cayenne

Vegetables:
taro root, celery, green onion, zucchini, snow peas, cherry tomatoes, asparagus spears, peppers (red, green, etc.), carrots.

Place all ingredients into a food processor and puree (a blender can be used). Place into an ice cream machine and ice according to manufacturer's instructions.

Serves 6

SUTTER HOME

CALIFORNIA
WHITE ZINFANDEL

MADE AND BOTTLED BY
SUTTER HOME WINERY BW 1007
ST. HELENA, CALIFORNIA
ALCOHOL 9% BY VOLUME

A fresh and fruity wine, soft and refreshing.

It is a perfect aperitif, and accompanies meat
and pasta dishes, and all light foods.

The Marshall House

~~~~~~~~~~~~~~~~~~~~~~

835 Second Street • Santa Rosa, California
(707) 542-5305
Hours: 11:30 a.m. - 2:30 p.m., Lunch
5:00 p.m. - 9:00 p.m., Dinner
4:00 p.m. - 9:00 p.m., Sunday Dinner
Closed Monday for Dinner
Credit Cards: Visa, M/C
Prices: Moderate
Reservations: Necessary
Specialties: German-style Home Cooking

~~~~~~~~~~~~~~~~~~~~~~

Enjoy all your favorite German specialties, like Sauerbraten, Potato Cakes and Spaetzle at Marshall House, just a few blocks from downtown in Santa Rosa. The home-style cooking is delicious, as you dine in this quiet restaurant overlooking a tree-lined street in the residential area of town. This popular spot fills up fast, so reservations are definitely a must.

113

Sauerbraten

For Marinade:
3 parts water
1 part red wine vinegar
carrots
celery
onions
juniper berries
bay leaves
ginger root

For Roasted Beef:
3 lbs. top round or lean bottom round beef

Marinade: Boil all ingredients for about 15 minutes. Strain and bring to room temperature. Put the meat in a plastic or stainless steel (not aluminum) pot or bowl and cover it with the marinade just enough to cover the meat. Keep in refrigerator for about 3-4 days. *Roasting of Beef:* Take the meat out of the marinade; dry it well with a towel (otherwise it will not brown when roasting) and do not season with salt (otherwise meat will fall apart too easily). Roast the meat in a 350° oven for about 2 hours. Take the meat out and cover it in a bowl with plastic wrap so it will not dry out. Prepare gravy (recipe follows).

Serves 6-8

Sauerbraten Gravy

2 T. tomato puree
white pepper
salt
2 T. flour
2 T. water
2 T. red wine

Take some of the stock from roasting the marinated beef and put it in a pot and add tomato puree, white pepper, salt and reduce it (cooking it down with constant stirring in order not to burn) until it starts to get dark brown. Repeat the same procedure 3 times and finally add part of the original marinade and some water. Let all boil and thicken it with diluted flour. Boil for a few minutes and take it off the heat. Season it and add red wine to enhance the flavor. Pour over meat and serve with potato pancakes.

Potato Pancakes

8 raw potatoes
2 onions
2 egg yolks
salt
pepper
nutmeg
4 T. vegetable oil

Peel and shred white potatoes and onions and put them in a strainer to get the water and starch out. Put the fairly dry mixture in a bowl and add egg yolks, salt, pepper and nutmeg. Heat oil in skillet and add potato mixture. Fry on both sides until golden brown. Drain well on paper towels, serve.

Serves 6-8

Rinder Rouladen
(Stuffed Beef Rolls)

1 lb. thinly sliced beef from top round (6 slices)
1 T. mustard
6 slices smoked bacon

Stuffing:
½ lb. ground beef
½ lb. ground pork
¼ t. each salt and pepper
½ t. caraway
¼ t. nutmeg
¼ t. marjoram
1 T. onion
1 t. pickle
1 T. cooked carrot

Pound beef; sprinkle with salt and cover with mustard. Place a slice of smoked bacon on top of the slice of beef; form a little ball of ground pork and beef (which has been thoroughly mixed with: salt, pepper, caraway, nutmeg, marjoram) and top it with fresh onion, pickle and cooked carrot. Roll beef slice carefully and string it in order to keep it together. In a fry pan with hot oil, brown beef rolls on all sides and put them in a pot with just enough water to cover. Boil for about 30 minutes over medium heat. Take beef roll out and prepare brown gravy from stock. Serve with homemade Spaetzle and red cabbage.

Serves 6

Spaetzle
(Flour Dumplings)

1 c. flour
¼ c. (or more) milk
¼ t. nutmeg
½ t. salt
2 eggs

Sift flour into a mixing bowl. Add milk, nutmeg, salt and eggs and mix all until smooth. Add salt and a bit of oil to boiling water. Place dough on a cutting board and, with a wet knife, cut little pieces into water. (You may also use a strainer with bigger holes to press dough through it into the water.) Let boil for a few minutes. Remove pot from stove and let stand for a while. Put spaetzle into a strainer and pour cold water over; let drain well. For serving, fry quickly in fry pan with butter.

RESTAURANT

Matisse

620 Fifth Street • Santa Rosa, California
(707) 527-9797
Hours: 11:30 a.m. - 2:00 p.m., Lunch, Monday-Friday
6:00 p.m. - 9:00 p.m., Dinner, Monday-Saturday
Credit Cards: Visa, M/C, A/X, D/C, C/B
Prices: Moderate
Reservations: Advised
Specialties: New French and New American Cuisine

New American and New French Cuisines served in an intimate dining room em-
bellished wth sparkling mirrors, fresh flowers and unusual and stunning prints by
Matisse await you at Matisse, located in downtown Santa Rosa. A different menu is
written each day using the freshest items offered at market, with specialties like grilled
fish, grilled Reichardt Petaluma Duck, and lobster salad with sliced roma tomatoes.
A wine list with more than 50 specially selected offerings including a number of
Sonoma County's most prestigious labels is available, with premium wines by the
glass. A number of ports and late-harvest wines are also served from the sophisticated
dessert menu.

Duck Liver Pate´

1 lb. duck livers
2 c. milk
6 egg yolks
1¼ c. whipping cream
½ lb. butter, melted
3 T. brandy
1½ t. salt
1½ t. freshly ground pepper
½ t. ground allspice

Soak livers in milk at least 1 hour or overnight. Pre-heat oven to 350°. Butter an 8½ x 4" glass loaf pan; line with cooking parchment to fit on top of loaf pan; set aside. Drain livers and discard milk. Trim livers of any fat or extraneous tissue. In a food processor, puree livers thoroughly along with egg yolks. Add cream and process again. Add butter, brandy and spices. The mixture will be quite liquid. Fill the prepared loaf pan with the liver mixture, then cover with buttered parchment. Set loaf pan in a 9 x 13" baking pan and add enough hot water to reach half way up the sides of the loaf pan. Bake for 60 to 75 minutes, or until the mixture sets and just barely juggles when shaken. Chill overnight in the refrigerator. To unmold, peel off the top paper. Dip the loaf pan in hot water and turn the pan over onto a cutting board or plate. Peel off paper. Slice; serve with French bread, gherkins, and Dijon mustard.

Serves 8-10

Filet of Salmon with Sorrel Sauce

1 stick butter
four 6-oz. salmon filets
½ c. white wine
1 T. minced shallot
½ c. fish stock (optional)
¼ c. heavy cream
½ c. sorrel, cut in strips

Heat butter in non-reactive skillet. Sear filets gently (don't brown) on both sides. Add wine and shallots to pan. Cover with lid or buttered waxed paper. Finish cooking in 375° oven or on top of stove over low heat. Remove fish from pan. Add fish stock (or more wine) and cream to pan. Reduce until thick and syrupy. Place fish on plates and then finish sauce. Swirl small chunks of butter into reduction. Warm gently if necessary, but do not allow butter to break. Stir in chopped sorrel and pour over fish.

Serves 4

Chocolate Marquise

8 oz. semi-sweet chocolate, cut in pieces
1 c. + 2 T. powdered sugar, sifted
6 oz. butter, room temperature
5 eggs, separated
¾ c. cocoa powder, sifted
dash of salt and cream of tartar
¾ c. whipping cream

Melt chocolate in double boiler over simmering water. Use electric mixer and add sugar. Mix in well. Add butter a little at a time, blending well after each addition. Remove from over simmering water and add egg yolk, one at a time, mixing well after each addition. Beat in cocoa. Let cool 5 minutes, stirring frequently. Meanwhile, beat egg whites with salt and tartar to stiff peaks. Stir ⅓ of the whites into chocolate mixture to lighten. Fold in the rest of the meringue. Beat cream to soft peaks. Fold into chocolate mixture until well blended. Chill in glass loaf pan at least 12 hours. To unmold, wet towel with hot water, invert loaf pan onto serving platter and wrap towel around it. Let sit a few seconds and tap pan firmly to loosen marquise. Slice into ten portions and serve with cream anglaise*.

Serves 10

* See Glossary

The Dining Room

1457 Lincoln Avenue • Calistoga, California
(707) 942-6877
Hours: 8:00 a.m. - 11:00 a.m., Breakfast
11:30 a.m. - 2:00 p.m., Lunch
6:00 p.m. - 9:00 p.m., Dinner
9:00 a.m. - 2:00 p.m., Sunday Brunch
Credit Cards: All Major
Prices: Moderate
Reservations: Recommended
Specialties: Wine Country Cuisine

At the Mount View the specialty is termed "Wine Country Cuisine" - an out-standing combination of game, seafood, pork or beef prepared using fresh products from the valley. Dine by the pool in the summer months or enjoy the art deco mixed with country designs in the dining room. Breakfast, lunch and dinner is served with Sunday brunch each week from 9:00 a.m. to 2:00 p.m. Located in the Mount View Hotel, there is a lot of entertainment every evening in the lounge and jazz bands at special times each month. Check out the calendar of events, too, for parties, wine tastings and gatherings.

Corn and Crayfish Chowder

12 ears of corn
4 lb. crayfish
¼ c. olive oil
1 onion
1 carrot
1 leek, roughly chopped
½ c. brandy
1½ c. white wine
seasoning

Slit kernels on the ears of corn. Scrape (do not cut) the kernels to get the juices out. Set aside. Blanch* crayfish in salted water; simmer 5 minutes. Chill under cold, running water. Remove meat from tails; save shells. Saute shells in olive oil. Add onion, carrot and leek. Continue sauteing. Deglaze* pan with brandy and white wine. Add enough water to cover the shells. Simmer for 2 hours. Strain off stock. Reduce to 3 cups liquid. Add scraped corn and bring back up to a boil. Check for seasoning. Garnish with crayfish tails.

* See Glossary

Rabbit with Merlot Sauce

1 medium rabbit
6 T. peanut oil
1 onion
2 stalks celery
1 carrot, finely diced
4 c. Merlot wine
chicken stock
2 bay leaves
1 T. thyme
salt and pepper

Have your butcher break down the rabbit into 6 pieces. Sear* the pieces until brown all over. Remove from the pan. Add a mire paix* of the onion, celery and carrot. Saute until tender. Deglaze* with 4 cups of Merlot wine and reduce. Add chicken stock, bay leaves and thyme; simmer. Place pieces of meat back in stock. Braise until tender, 45 minutes to 1 hour; remove meat. Strain off stock and reduce until it thickens. Season with salt and pepper.

Serves 2

* See Glossary

Chocolate Mousse Torte
with Almond Crust

Crust:
½ c. butter
1 c. flour
½ c. sugar
½ c. almonds (slivered, chopped and basted)

Torte:
1 lb. semi-sweet chocolate
2 eggs
4 egg yolks
2 c. whipping cream
6 T. powdered sugar
4 egg whites

Crust: Melt butter in large skillet. Stir in flour, sugar and almonds. Cook over medium heat. Stir constantly until mixture is golden brown and crumbly, 6 to 8 minutes. Press into a 10-inch springform pan. *Torte:* Soften chocolate in double boiler; cool. Add whole eggs and mix well. Add yolks and mix thoroughly. Whip cream with powdered sugar. Beat egg whites until stiff, not dry. Fold into chocolate mixture. Pour into crust. Chill 6 hours before serving.

Serves 8

Oakmont Inn

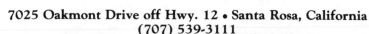

7025 Oakmont Drive off Hwy. 12 • Santa Rosa, California
(707) 539-3111
Hours: 9:00 a.m. - 1:00 p.m., Sunday Breakfast
9:00 a.m. - 3:00 p.m., Sunday Brunch
11:00 a.m. - 3:00 p.m., Mon. - Sat., Lunch
5:00 p.m. - 9:00 p.m., Mon. - Sat., Dinner
From 3:00 p.m., Sunday Dinner
Credit Cards: Visa, M/C, A/X
Prices: Moderate
Reservations: Suggested
Specialties: Continental

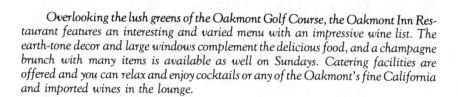

Overlooking the lush greens of the Oakmont Golf Course, the Oakmont Inn Restaurant features an interesting and varied menu with an impressive wine list. The earth-tone decor and large windows complement the delicious food, and a champagne brunch with many items is available as well on Sundays. Catering facilities are offered and you can relax and enjoy cocktails or any of the Oakmont's fine California and imported wines in the lounge.

127

Prawns Amoureuse

½ T. diced shallots
6 medium sliced mushrooms
1 T. diced bell pepper
1 T. butter
10 peeled & deveined prawns
salt and pepper to taste
½ medium peeled tomato
1 T. capers
chopped garlic
tarragon
chervil
cayenne
1 shot brandy
½ shot Pernod
1 c. heavy cream
chopped parsley

Saute shallots, mushrooms and bell peppers in butter; add prawns, seasoned with salt and pepper, tomatoes, capers, garlic, tarragon, chervil, and a touch of cayenne pepper. Stir over brisk heat, then flame with brandy and Pernod. Add heavy cream and let reduce to desired thickness. Sprinkle with chopped parsley and serve with rice. Herbs and spices should be used to the individual's taste.

Serves 2

Medallions of Veal "Maxim"

4 veal medallions, approx. 3 oz. each
salt
paprika
flour
butter
1 c. sliced mushrooms
1 shot brandy
1 shot Port wine
¾ c. extra heavy cream

Season veal with salt and paprika. Dip in flour and saute in skillet with butter until desired doneness. Add mushrooms and flame with brandy and Port wine. Remove veal; add cream and reduce to proper thickness. Pour over medallions and serve with rice or noodles.

Serves 2

Flan Florentine

2 puff pastry sheets, 7" x 14"
2 breasts of capon or chicken
salt
pepper
flour
1 T. diced onion
1 T. butter
1 c. spinach, blanched and chopped
2 thick slices Sonoma Jack cheese

Bake puff pastry sheets and carefully remove the center, creating a rectangular patty shell. Season chicken with salt and pepper, dip in flour and brown chicken on both sides. Remove when half done. Saute onions in butter, add spinach and season with salt and pepper. Place spinach in puff pastry, top with chicken breast and cover with slice of Sonoma Jack. Bake for 15 minutes at 375°. Serve.

Serves 2

The Penguins Fish Grotto
Restaurant

1533 Trancas Street • Napa, California
(707) 252-4343
Hours: 11:30 a.m. - 2:30 p.m., Lunch, Monday-Friday
4:30 p.m. - 9:30 p.m., Dinner, Monday-Saturday
Closed Sunday
Credit Cards: Visa, M/C, A/X
Prices: Moderate
Reservations: Suggested
Specialties: Seafood

The freshest seafood and produce available is delivered for preparation each day to The Penguins Fish Grotto in Napa for choice seafood dishes and salads. The menu has many delicious shellfish, lobster, and fish dishes from which to choose, and an uncluttered wine list using labels from surrounding wineries. The decor at The Penguins is enhanced by subdued lighting using wall sconces between the red leather booths and richly-flocked brocaded wallpaper all around. The Penguins is open for lunch and dinner and is closed on Sundays.

Bouillabaisse Fisherman's Style

There are various ingredients and methods used in preparing this elegant soup/stew from the Marseilles area of France. Rather than join the controversy, this American version was created to make use of the fish that are plentiful in this part of the world.

3 medium onions, coarsely chopped
3-4 garlic cloves, chopped
1 c. olive oil
8 oz. red wine
5-6 ripe tomatoes, peeled and chopped in cubes
2 small hot chili peppers, seeded and chopped
1 leek, chopped
¼ c. parsley, chopped
¼ bunch fresh cilantro
¼ t. black pepper
¼ t. red hot pepper
1 bay leaf
½ t. saffron
¼ c. dry, whole grain bread crumbs
salt to taste
4 c. fish stock
2 lb. combination of: rock cod, snapper, halibut and sea bass
1 lb. scallops
1 lb. prawns, shelled
12 cherrystone clams
12 mussels
2 Dungeness crabs
  (use claws and legs only)

Bouillabaisse Fisherman's Style (Cont.)

In sauce pan over medium heat, saute onions and garlic in olive
oil. Add red wine and diced tomatoes and saute for 10 minutes.
Add all the other ingredients (except fish stock and fish); mix
well. Add fish stock and simmer for 30 minutes. Add rock cod,
snapper, halibut and sea bass, all cleaned and cut into 1½" cubes.
Add scallops, prawns, clams, mussels and crab claws and legs.
Simmer until mussels and clams are opened.

Serves 10-12

Shrimp a la Creole

1 large onion, julienned
2 green peppers, julienned
½ c. butter
2 garlic cloves, finely minced
4 large, ripe tomatoes, peeled and diced
1 c. coarsely chopped celery
1 bay leaf
3 sprigs fresh thyme (or ¼ t. dried)
½ t. light honey
½ t. fresh parsley, chopped
3 slices lemon rind, shredded
2 lb. shrimp

Saute onions and green pepper in butter for 5 minutes. Add garlic. Add tomatoes and cook for 15 minutes. Add the rest of the ingredients (except shrimp) and cook for 5 more minutes. Add 2 pounds of shrimp meat and cook for 10 minutes.

Serves 6

Halibut or Sea Bass Mediterranean Style

½ c. olive oil
1 onion, chopped
4 garlic cloves, minced
4 t. flour
3 large tomatoes, diced
1 t. tomato paste
1 bunch parsley (chop the leaves, save stems)
3 c. fish stock
1 bay leaf
½ t. black pepper
salt to taste
3 lb. filet-style halibut or sea bass
2 T. butter
1 c. white wine
sliced tomatoes

Place saucepan on medium heat. Add olive oil, onion and garlic and saute until onion is clear. Add flour; mix well and then add tomatoes, tomato paste, fish stock, parsley stems, bay leaf, pepper and salt to taste. Boil for 20-30 minutes, stirring frequently. Cut halibut or sea bass into 2-3" filets. Place butter in baking pan. Place the filets in a single layer. Pour sauce over top. Add the wine and one thin slice of tomato on each filet. Sprinkle with parsley and bake in 400° oven for 15 minutes.

Serves 6

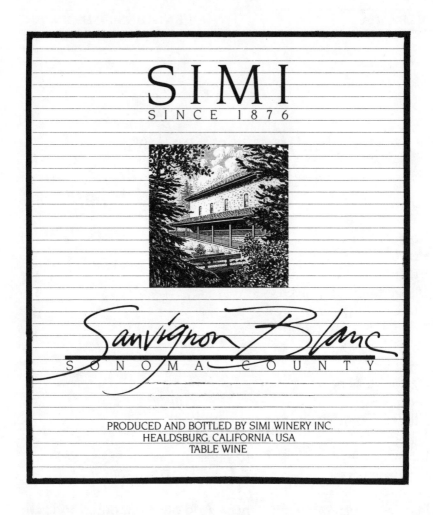

SIMI

SINCE 1876

Sauvignon Blanc

SONOMA COUNTY

PRODUCED AND BOTTLED BY SIMI WINERY INC.
HEALDSBURG, CALIFORNIA, USA
TABLE WINE

A lively wine with floral notes, spice, some oak and the sweet smell of hay.
Citrus and melon flavors, with a soft, mouth-filling texture.

Food affinities: Prawns and shrimp - fresh crab - oysters - goat cheeses -
Pasta Primavera

Plaza grill

109A Plaza Street • Healdsburg, California
(707) 431-8305
Hours: 11:30 a.m. - 2:00 p.m., Lunch, Monday-Saturday
5:30 p.m. - 9:00 p.m., Dinner, Monday-Thursday
5:30 p.m. - 9:30 p.m., Dinner, Friday & Saturday
Closed Sunday
Credit Cards: Visa, M/C
Prices: Moderate
Reservations: Suggested
Specialties: Mesquite Broiled Meat & Seafood

A new dinner menu is written each evening at Plaza Grill in Healdsburg to provide diners with fresh, local ingredients and new tastes to choose from. Dining here is intimate, with a wine bar and an award-winning local wine list. Specialties of the house are the mesquite-broiled meat and seafood dishes like fresh reef shark, lamb chops and Prawns Orley. The appetizers are creative and special, as are the salads and soups, all at moderate prices.

Apple Walnut Gorgonzola Salad

1 apple (Rome or Pippin)
1 head lettuce
2 oz. Gorgonzola cheese
2 oz. walnuts, coarsely chopped
raspberry vinaigrette (recipe follows)
fresh raspberries for garnish

Core apple and slice into thin wedges. On a bed of lettuce, arrange apple slices in a circle. Place crumbled Gorganzola in center of circle. Sprinkle with walnuts. Drizzle about 1 oz. of vinaigrette over salad. Garnish with fresh raspberries.

Serves 4

Raspberry Vinaigrette

12 oz. raspberry vinegar
4 oz. walnut oil
8 oz. vegetable oil
1 t. sugar
orange zest

Combine all ingredients and shake well.

Mushrooms Lorenzo

32 medium-large mushrooms
½ lb. bay shrimp
1 stalk celery
32 mushroom stems
1 T. parsley, chopped
¼ c. bechamel sauce*
¼ c. butter
1 c. hollandaise sauce*
1 T. parmesan cheese
1 T. parsley
paprika for garnish

Wash and stem mushrooms. Set caps aside. Chop shrimp, celery and mushroom stems. Add chopped parsley and bechamel sauce and mix. Spoon mixture into mushroom caps. Place mushroom caps in buttered 9" x 12" pan and bake at 475° for 10-12 minutes. Transfer to serving plate and top with hot hollandaise sauce, parmesan cheese, parsley and paprika.

Serves 4

* See Glossary

Pork Tenderloin with Pinot Noir Sauce

juice from 1 lemon
2 pork tenderloins
pepper
garlic powder
4 oz. Pinot Noir Sauce (recipe follows)
¼ green apple, cored

Squeeze ½ lemon over each pork tenderloin; sprinkle with fresh ground pepper and garlic powder. Broil over mesquite or in broiler. Place 1 oz. Pinot Noir sauce on each plate. Place ½ tenderloin on each plate. Make 3 diagonal slices in each piece of meat, almost all the way through. Place an apple slice in each cut.

Serves 4

Pinot Noir Sauce

2 limes
2 c. Pinot Noir
1 T. fresh ginger, sliced
½ c. honey
2 T. cornstarch
2 T. water

Squeeze lime. Combine lime juice, Pinot Noir and ginger over high heat and reduce by half; strain. Add honey; return to heat. Blend cornstarch and water together and thicken sauce with this mixture.

Silverado Restaurant
Calistoga, Napa Valley

Lincoln and Washington • Calistoga, California
(707) 942-6725
Hours: 7:00 a.m. - 3:00 p.m., Breakfast and Lunch
5:00 p.m. - 10:00 p.m., Dinner
Credit Cards: None
Prices: Moderate
Reservations: Advised
Specialties: Creative American Cooking

An eclectic menu with an outstanding wine list of more than 1100 selections is featured at the Silverado in Calistoga. The menu changes daily with delicious home-made soups, breads, and pastas to choose from, or any of the Silverado's entrees, which often include roast duckling, fresh fish, pork, seafood, quesadill and the Silverado Super Burger. Hand-painted local artworks adorn the wooden walls, as does a collection of interesting wine bottles of every description, set high on a shelf above the dining room.

141

Cherry Tomato and
Fresh Mussel Salad

2 lb. cherry tomatoes, steamed in ¼ c. white wine
1 bunch parsley
2 T. chopped garlic
2 lb. mussels, steamed & shelled, with cooking liquid reserved
¼ c. olive oil
⅞ c. champagne vinegar   ***
¼ c. hazelnut oil
mussel cooking liquid

Mix all ingredients in a bowl and chill thoroughly for at least two hours. Serve well chilled.

Sauteed Milk-fed Veal with Hazelnut Sauce

18 milk-fed veal scallops
4 T. unsalted butter
2 shallots, minced
1 clove garlic, minced
2 T. hazelnut oil
½ c. Sauvignon Blanc or dry Chenin Blanc
¼ c. ground and roasted hazelnuts
1 c. stock
2 T. Frangelico (hazelnut liqueur)
½ c. creme fraiche or heavy cream
salt and fresh ground pepper to taste

Saute the veal, just before you plan to serve it, in the butter. Remove from pan and place on warm plate to keep warm. Leave saute pan on burner and add shallots and garlic; saute until golden. Then place hazelnut oil, white wine, nuts and stock into pan and reduce by one half. Add the Frangelico and cream and reduce again by one half. Season with salt and pepper. Arrange the veal on a serving platter or individual plates and pour the sauce over the veal.

Bouillabaisse

3 red bell peppers, diced
3 green bell pepper, diced
1 onion, diced
1 T. chopped garlic
⅓ c. olive oil
1 T. saffron
pinch of thyme
pinch of rosemary
salt and pepper to taste
1 gallon fish stock
1 lb. mussels
1 lb. clams
1 lb. snapper
1 lb. crayfish or prawns
½ lb. fresh tuna
½ lb. swordfish
zest of one lemon
zest of one orange

Sweat the peppers, onion and garlic in the olive oil. Add herbs and simmer. When thoroughly cooked, puree in a food processor. Bring fish stock to a boil. Add the vegetable mixture. Add the shellfish and cook until they open. Add the remaining seafood. Toss in the citrus zests at the end. Ladle the seafood into a bowl and pour the fish stock over it. Serve with Rouille (recipe follow) and French bread toasts.

Serves 8-10

Rouille (Cayenne Aioli)

3 egg yolks
pinch of saffron
2 T. garlic puree
1 T. cayenne
1 T. tomato puree
salt and pepper to taste
1½ c. olive oil

Place egg yolks in a food processor or blender. Add saffron, garlic, cayenne, tomato puree, salt and white pepper. Beat at high speed and add olive oil slowly in a stream, drop by drop, to form a thick emulsion. Spread on the toasts or serve on the side for everyone to add to the bouillabaisse.

Napa Valley

CABERNET SAUVIGNON

Vintage   *Jack Schulze,*
Proprietaire

Napa Creek Winery

ALCOHOL 13.3% BY VOLUME

PRODUCED AND BOTTLED BY NAPA CREEK WINERY
ST. HELENA, NAPA VALLEY, CALIFORNIA

A mellow cabernet with a nice hint of raspberry on the nose
and finished with a smooth and slight oak taste.

Recommended as a companion to steak or lamb.

SONOMA MISSION INN AND SPA

18140 Sonoma Highway 12 • Boyes Hot Springs, California
(707) 938-9000
Hours: 8:00 a.m. - 10:30 a.m., Breakfast
11:30 a.m. - 3:00 p.m., Lunch
6:00 p.m. - 10:00 p.m., Dinner
Credit Cards: All Major
Prices: Moderate
Reservations: Recommended & Required on Weekends
Specialties: Spa & Wine Country Cuisine

An innovative menu of wine country cuisine, using only the finest in fresh vegetables and food products is found at the Sonoma Mission Inn and Spa. The new grille restaurant, enlarged and remodeled with skylights and a crisp, casual feeling, offers an imaginative menu accompanied by an impressive wine list of 140 Sonoma Valley wines. Breakfast, lunch and dinner is served with menu items prepared with Sonoma cheese and sausages, local baby vegetables, fresh local seafood and much more. Pure linen tablecloths and fresh cut flowers on each table add the finishing touches at this moderately priced restaurant.

Plum Smoked Salmon

1 lb. salmon filet
plum wood

Cure:
4 oz. salt
4 oz. sugar
⅙ c. dill weed, chopped

Oil:
1 pt. cottonseed oil
½ c. dill stems

Marinade:
2 scallions
1 c. orange juice
2 cloves garlic, chopped
1 T. brown sugar
¼ c. olive oil

Spread salt and sugar "cure" mixture evenly over both sides of salmon filet. Leave overnight or 10 hours. Rinse filet under cold water to remove all "cure" mixture. Submerge filet in oil and dill mixture overnight or 10 hours. Remove filet from oil and pat dry with paper towels. Marinate filet for 3 hours in marinade. Smoke over cool home barbecue or smoker containing plum wood at 55° for 30 minutes or until firm to the touch. Serve at room temperature with lemon, daikon, and cucumber with dill.

Serves 4

Souverain Restaurant
at the Winery

Independence Lane • Geyserville, California
(707) 433-3141
Hours: 11:00 a.m. - 3:00 p.m., Lunch, Monday-Saturday
5:30 p.m. - 9:30 p.m., Dinner, Friday & Saturday
5:30 p.m. - 9:00 p.m., Dinner, Wednesday, Thursday & Sunday
Closed Monday and Tuesday for Dinner
10:30 a.m. - 2:30 p.m., Sunday Brunch
Credit Cards: Visa, M/C, A/X, D/C
Prices: Moderate
Reservations: Required
Specialties: Continental (New California Cuisine)

Set overlooking the Souverain Vineyards, the Souverain Restaurant is truly beautiful with its outdoor courtyard and fountain, warm, gracious interior dining area and wood paneling. New California Cuisine, ranging from seafood to steaks, a seafood buffet offered each Friday, and champagne brunch buffet on Sundays with flowing wine and champagne are always favorites. The restaurant is open for lunch and dinner, and in the warm months, dining is available on the outdoor terrace with a panoramic view of the surrounding wine country.

149

French Onion Soup

4 medium onions
1 T. butter
1 c. Souverain Chablis
1 qt. beef broth
salt and pepper to taste
round toast with parmesan cheese
2 slices Swiss cheese

Slice onions thin and brown in butter. Add Souverain Chablis and reduce to half. Add broth and salt and pepper to taste. Simmer until onions are tender. Arrange toast on top of soup, layer cheese slices over toast and broil until cheese melts. Serve hot.

Serves 4

Profiteroles au Chocolate

½ c. shortening
salt to taste
1 c. boiling water
1 c. sifted flour
3 unbeaten eggs
vanilla ice cream
chocolate sauce
brandy to taste

Add shortening and salt to boiling water and stir over medium heat until mixture boils; lower heat. Add flour all at once and stir vigorously until mixture leaves the sides of the the pan. Remove from heat and add eggs, one at a time, beating thoroughly after each addition. Shape on an ungreased cookie sheet, using 1 T. for each puff. Bake in hot oven (450°) for 20 minutes. Reduce temperature to 350° and bake another 20 minutes. Let cool completely. Make slit on each side and fill with vanilla ice cream. Serve on a plate with hot chocolate and brandy.

Makes 12 puffs

Souverain Cheesecake

Crust:
2 c. graham cracker crumbs
⅝ c. sugar
¾ c. melted butter

Filling:
1½ lb. cream cheese
1 c. sugar
3 eggs
1 oz. butter
1 t. orange extract

Combine cracker crumbs, sugar and butter. Pour crumb mixture into a springform pan and press crumbs into bottom. *Filling:* Beat cream cheese; add sugar. Gradually add eggs, one at a time. Add butter and extract. Pour into pan with crust mixture and bake at 450° for 30 minutes. Let cool completely. Remove from pan; slice and serve.

Starmont Restaurant

900 Meadowood Lane • St. Helena, California
(707) 963-3646
Hours: 7:30 a.m. - 10:30 p.m., Breakfast
11:30 a.m. - 2:30 p.m., Lunch
6:00 p.m. - 9:00 p.m., Dinner
Credit Cards: All Major
Prices: Moderate-Expensive
Reservations: Suggested
Specialties: Seafood

Winner of the prestigious Golden Fork Award from the International Food, Wine and Travel Writers Association, the Starmont Restaurant is fast becoming well-known for its exclusive dining accommodations and culinary delights. The freshest seafood highlights the menu, as do the chef's specialty desserts. The restaurant overlooks the beautiful and scenic Meadowood Golf Course, creating an intimate setting for fine dining. Executive conference facilities are available as well. The menu, created by one of California's top chefs, Hale Lake, changes every night with a prix fixe selection and a la carte choices. Eighty percent of the produce used in preparing the Starmont's delectable dishes is grown on the property, or in close proximity. There is also an herb garden, grown specially for many of the Starmont's menu items, to bring out the liveliest and most aromatic of flavors.

153

Wild Mushroom and Ginger Soup with Chervil Leaves

¾ lb. cepes, chanterelles, bolitis, or other wild mushrooms*
2 T. butter
2 T. peanut oil
2 small garlic cloves
1 T. ginger, peeled and grated
2 small shallots
salt and cayenne
3 c. heavy cream
¼ lemon, juiced
5 sprigs chervil

Clean and trim the mushrooms and mince them along with the garlic and shallots. Remove the leaves of chervil from the stems to yield 2 to 3 teaspoons of leaves. In a frying pan over high heat, add the minced mushrooms; when they have rendered their juices, add the butter, oil, garlic, ginger, shallots, salt and pepper; mix together and continue cooking until the mushrooms are nicely browned. Remove half of the mushroom mixture from the pan and reserve as a garnish. Add the cream to the remaining half of the mushroom mixture. Scrape the bottom of the pan to remove any cooked-on juices and then pour the mixture into a sauce pan. Bring to a boil for two minutes. Remove from heat and puree in a food processor. Put the mushroom puree into a sauce pan; thin it with water until it reaches the consistency of thick soup, and season it with salt, cayenne and lemon juice to taste. Now bring it

154

Wild Mushroom & Ginger Soup (Cont.)

to a boil and keep warm. Ladle the soup into small bowls. Put 1/6 of the mushroom garnish in the center of each serving and then sprinkle the chervil over the soup.

* 1½ oz. (about 1½ c.) dried cepes, first soaked in warm water for at least half an hour, can be used in place of fresh mushrooms.

Serves 6

Fresh Cured Salmon with Lemon-Thyme Vinaigrette

2 lb. center cut fresh King, Atlantic or Chinook salmon
¼ c. sea salt
½ c. brown sugar
1 bunch fresh dill, coarsely chopped
2 t. crushed white peppercorns

Scale and debone the salmon, cutting the fish into two pieces along the line of the backbone. Do not rinse the pieces, but wipe dry with paper towels. Mix salt and sugar and rub fish with the mixture. Sprinkle part of the mixture and some of the dill in an earthenware baking dish. Place one piece of salmon, skin side down, in the dish and sprinkle generously with dill, crushed peppercorns, and salt/sugar mixture. Cover with the second piece of salmon, skin side up. If the pieces do not match in shape, place the thick side against the thin side. Sprinkle the salmon with remaining salt/sugar mixture. Cover with a sheet of aluminum foil and a light weight. Keep the fish refrigerated for at least 48 hours, turning over at least twice during that period. It can be stored for a week if properly chilled. To serve, cut into very thin slices from from the skin. Garnish with California golden caviar and sliced cucumbers. Pour on Lemon-Thyme Vinaigrette (recipe follows).

Lemon-Thyme Vinaigrette

¾ c. oil (50% virgin olive oil, 50% hazelnut oil)
3 lemons, juiced
2 t. lemon-thyme, chopped with no stems
1 T. balsamic vinegar

In a bowl, combine all ingredients and blend well.

Loin of Milk-Fed Veal with Pancetta & Basil, Port Wine & Orange Sauce

2 lb. of milk-fed veal, loin cut, trimmed & silverskin removed
12 oz. sheet of pancetta* (about 1/3 of a slice)
12 leaves of purple, lemon or green basil
   (can substitute fresh sage or other stronger herbs, to permeate)
fresh ground white pepper
string
2 T. olive oil

Lay sheet of pancetta on a cutting board and place basil leaves down the center of pancetta. Place loin of veal out to leaves and season well with white pepper. Roll pancetta as to wrap the veal loin inside of it and secure by tieing with string from left to right with 1½" to 2" space between each tie. In a saute pan, over high heat, place veal wrapped in pancetta into it and sear** on all sides. Place in 350° oven for 25 minutes. Remove from oven and let stand for five minutes. Slice ½" thick slices before removing string. (Chances of pancetta unraveling are slimmer.) Then remove string from each portion. To serve, place 2 oz. of port and orange sauce (recipe follows) on a dinner plate. Then place sliced veal in pancetta onto sauce.

Serves 8

* A type of ham, available in specialty food shops.

** See Glossary

158

Port and Orange Sauce

3 c. Port wine
½ c. orange juice
4 c. strong beef or veal stock
½ c. cream
salt and pepper to taste

Reduce Port wine by half. Add orange juice, beef or veal stock and again, reduce by half. Add cream and season.

SILVERADO HILL CELLARS

NAPA VALLEY
CHARDONNAY

PRODUCED & ESTATE BOTTLED BY SILVERADO HILL CELLARS
NAPA, CALIFORNIA • ALCOHOL 13.0% BY VOL. • CONTAINS SULFITES

Character of Wine: Variety true fragrance derived from the grape, oaky montrachet bouquet from winemaking method.

Food pairing: Goes well with seafood and poultry.

1075 California Boulevard • Napa, California
(707) 253-9540
Hours: 11:00 a.m. - 3:00 p.m., Lunch, Mon.-Fri.
5:00 p.m. - 11:00 p.m., Dinner, Mon.-Fri.
11:00 a.m. - 11:00 p.m., Sat. & Sun.
Credit Cards: Visa, M/C, A/X, D/C
Prices: Moderate
Reservations: Recommended
Specialties: California Cuisine

Dining at the Swan Court Cage in the Embassy Suites Hotel of Napa is definitely an experience not to be missed. With its large atrium dining room, lavish greenery, high, high ceilings and large ficas trees, the Swan Court is an architectural masterpiece and a true dining pleasure. The meandering pool with goldfish, ornamental Japanese Koi and ducks is bordered by several dining tables and there are two gazebos with charm of their own. The menu, created by Executive Chef, Matthew A. di Sabella, a graduate of the Culinary Institute of America in Hyde Park, is California cuisine with many items to choose from at lunch or dinner. Cafe specialties like baby back ribs, fresh fish or duck are listed on the menu, as are many salad creations, steaks and much more.

161

BBQ Baby Back Ribs

1½ lbs. baby back ribs
kosher salt
cracked black pepper
paprika
chili powder
tumeric
onion powder
granulated garlic
ground cumin

Peel off the thin membrane on the inside portion of the ribs. Mix equal parts of seasonings together and season both sides of ribs. Hang ribs in smoker oven at 250°. Use grape wood only. Put a pan of water in the bottom for steam. Be sure to replenish grape wood chips as they burn, to keep a nice even thick smoke, for 45 minutes. Remove ribs and dip in BBQ sauce (recipe follows). Return them to smoker for another 45 minutes or until tender. Cut between ribs before serving.

Serves 4

BBQ Sauce

2 T. Poupon Dijon mustard
1 c. tomato puree
¼ c. brown sugar
½ c. distilled vinegar
1 T. grapeseed oil
1 T. minced onion
1 T. minced garlic
salt to taste

Blend all ingredients together and simmer for 20 minutes.

"Fajitas"
(Sizzling Skirt Steak)

1 6-ounce skirt steak
salt and pepper to taste
2 T. salad oil
1 t. lime juice
1 t. oil
3 oz. sliced white onion
1 t. oil
3 flour tortillas

Trim all fat and remove skin from steak. Season with salt and pepper on both sides and let it marinate in salad oil and lime juice overnight. Broil over mesquite charcoal until rare. Slice thinly against grain. Transfer to hot saute pan together with the oil and sliced white onion. Toss for 1 minute. Place an iron skillet on a separate burner to get hot (not too hot or the fajitas will burn). Turn off burner and add oil, the sliced steak and onions. Serve immediately. Serve with flour tortillas that have been warmed on an open burner or griddle. As a topping, use guacamole, sour cream, grated cheese, and Pico de Gallo (recipe follows).

Pico de Gallo

3 T. diced onion
3 T. diced tomatoes
salt and pepper to taste
1 T. chopped cilantro

Mix all ingredients and chill.

Shrimp in Beer Batter

Clean and devein the shrimp, and cut down the back, keeping the tail shell attached. Sprinkle shrimp with lemon juice. Dip shrimp into flour and then into beer batter (recipe follows).

Beer Batter

12 oz. Heineken beer
1 c. sifted all purpose flour
1 t. salt
1 t. paprika
1 pinch baking powder

Combine all ingredients, stirring with a wire whisk. Hold the floured shrimp by the tail and dip into batter. Allow the excess batter to drain off, and deep fry shrimp until golden brown and crisp, about 5 minutes at 375°. Drain and serve immediately, garnished with cilantro and serve with orange and ginger sauce (recipe follows).

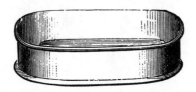

Orange and Ginger Sauce

¾ c. orange marmalade
4 T. lemon juice
2 T. orange juice
1 T. prepared horseradish
½ t. powdererd ginger
pinch of salt
½ t. English mustard
pinch of white pepper

Place all ingredients in a blender for 15 seconds. Use to accompany beer batter shrimp or as a dipping sauce for raw vegetables.

RESTAURANT & BAR

6539 Washington Street • Yountville, California
(707) 944-2406
Hours: 11:30 a.m. - 5:30 p.m., Lunch
From 5:30 p.m., Dinner
From 9:30 a.m., Brunch, Saturday & Sunday
Credit Cards: Visa, M/C, A/X
Prices: Moderate
Reservations: Not Required
Specialties: California-American Cuisine

"A tribute to the past and reminder of another era" is printed on the back of the menu of the Washington Street Restaurant, which truly is a unique place, especially for history buffs. From the 100-year-old back bar to the brick and leaded glass surroundings, this old mansion is lovely to behold, situated with a view of the vineyards. Dining is offered inside and outside, with a menu of California and American cuisine. Enjoy piano entertainment nightly, full bar service and an extensive wine list as well, and don't miss the homemade gelato - ice cream at its finest.

167

Walnut Vinaigrette

12 oz. walnut oil
¼ c. salad oil
7 oz. red wine vinegar
½ t. sugar
½ t. salt
pinch white pepper
2 t. parsley, chopped

Refrigerate the oils for at least 3 hours. Remove from the refrigerator and blend slowly into the remaining combined ingredients. Refrigerate once again before using.

Makes 3 cups

Curried King Salmon Filet served with Mango & Ginger-Lime Sauce

5 6-oz. salmon filets
4 oz. curry
3 oz. clarified butter *
1 medium mango, pureed
8 limes, juiced
2 oz. ginger, grated
salt and pepper to taste
8 oz. butter chips, unsalted

Dredge the salmon filets in 3 oz. of curry and saute in clarified butter on both sides until done. Remove salmon from pan and leave in warm place. Add mango, lime juice, ginger, salt and pepper, and one ounce of curry to pan. Reduce by half and remove from heat. Whip in the butter chips and season to taste. Place salmon on top of the sauce when ready to serve.

Serves 6

* See Glossary

CAYMUS VINEYARDS

NAPA VALLEY

Sauvignon Blanc

PRODUCED AND BOTTLED BY
CAYMUS VINEYARDS
RUTHERFORD, NAPA VALLEY, CA.
ALCOHOL 13.0% BY VOLUME

Very fresh and fruity, highly-flavored style of this varietal, with just a hint of the "grassy" Sauvignon character.

Matches extraordinarily with Asparagus Hollandaise and lemon poultry dishes.

Added Attractions

VINTAGED
NAPA VALLEY

CHARDONNAY

PRODUCED AND BOTTLED BY
FREEMARK ABBEY WINERY, ST. HELENA, CALIFORNIA, U.S.A.
Alcohol 13.0% by volume

Bold, dramatic, full-bodied wine! Excellent bottle bouquet. Intense fruit flavors.

Delicious with seafood, salads, poultry and pastas.

NAPA VALLEY
BALLOONS, INC.

P.O. Box 2860 • Yountville, California 94599
1 (800) 253-2224 or (707) 253-2224

What could be more beautiful than a balloon ride over the magnificent Napa Valley in the morning, followed by a delicious champagne picnic, complete with all the trimmings? Napa Valley Balloons offers a complete mornings' adventure over the vineyards and meadows of the valley each day (weather permitting) usually between 6 and 8 a.m. After your hot air balloon ride, which lasts about an hour, you'll be treated to a great picnic of cheese, salami, crackers, French bread, dips and pastries, and, of course, plenty of champagne. Guests also receive an instant color photo of their lift-off or landing and a balloon pin, depicting the balloon they flew. It's a fun experience, happening year-round, with launches from various spots in the scenic Napa Valley.

173

Salsa

5-6 medium tomatoes, cubed
2 green chilies, fresh
½ bunch cilantro
6 or 7 tomatillas, chopped
1 medium yellow onion, chopped
salt to taste

Mix all ingredients together. Serve with tortilla chips.

Pate' Dip

8 oz. braunschweiger
½ pt. sour cream
½ c. parsley
4 drops tabasco sauce

Mix all ingredients well. Serve with crackers.

Stuffed Cherry Tomatoes

1 basket cherry tomatoes
2 cans deviled ham
3 pickles, chopped
mayonnaise

Core tomatoes. Mix rest of ingredients together and stuff tomatoes.

Quiche Lorraine

1 pie crust
1 T. salad oil
¾ c. fresh mushrooms, sliced
1 c. thinly sliced onion
1 c. grated Swiss cheese
6 strips bacon, cooked crisp, drained
1 can water chestnuts, quartered
3 eggs, beaten
2 c. half & half
½ t. salt
½ t. white pepper
¼ t. ground nutmeg

Preheat oven to 400°. Bake pie crust for 8 minutes and set aside.
Increase oven to 450°. In a skillet, add salad oil and saute mushrooms and onion. Cover bottom of pie crust with cheese, onion
and mushroom mixture, bacon and water chestnuts. Mix eggs,
half & half, salt, pepper and nutmeg. Pour over ingredients in pie
crust. Bake at 450° for 10 minutes. Reduce oven to 350° and
cook for 20 minutes more. Serve hot or cold.

Serves 8

Groth

Napa Valley Chardonnay

CELLARED AND BOTTLED BY GROTH VINEYARDS
RUTHERFORD, CALIFORNIA   ALC. 13.5% BY VOL.

Rich with toasty, creamy oak and a nice balance of lemon citrus and apple fruit aromas and flavors.

Food pairing: Grilled chicken breasts with fresh avocado salsa or roasted pork tenderloin with a mustard cream sauce.

7856 St. Helena Highway • Oakville, California
(707) 944-8802
Credit Cards: Visa/ M/C, A/X

You won't find many grocery stores like this one - known all around for its "innovative and eclectic California style." Strands of garlic, spices, and salami hang from the ceiling and counters where you'll find delicious and wonderful picnic foods, cheeses and lots of local wines. Order from the courteous help for a super lunch or picnic, or buy what you'd like and create your own delicious meal. The fresh pasta, hot radicchio salad and sushi all can be purchased right from the grocery for a unique taste sensation. No matter what you decide, it's a definite experience to shop here and one you won't want to miss while in California wine country.

177

California Sushi Roll

1 pkg. (or 7 sheets) toasted nori (Japanese seaweed) *
5 c. pearl or sushi rice *
½ c. rice vinegar *
5 T. sugar
2 t. salt
2 ripe avocados
1 small cucumber
soy sauce for dipping
wasabe (Japanese horseradish) for dipping
1-2 T. flying fish roe or golden caviar (optional)

Equipment helpful, but not essential: a bamboo sushi rolling mat.

Wash rice in cold water. Drain it and allow to sit for 2 hours. Combine the rice with 5 cups cold water in a pot. Place on medium-high to high heat. Cover and allow to come to a boil. Do not remove lid or stir. Reduce the heat to low and cook for 20 minutes until tender. Meanwhile, mix together the rice vinegar, sugar and salt. Turn the hot rice into a large bowl; pour the vinegar mixture over, and stir occasionally, allowing it to cool as quickly as possible. To assemble, lay one sheet of nori with a short side closest to you on the bamboo mat. Spread about 1½ c. rice over the nori, leaving an uncovered strip at the edge away from you of about 2". The rice should be an approximate square. Peel and slice the avocado and cucumber and place a wedge of each across the rice in the center. Carefully fold the bamboo mat or damp towel up around the rice, using it as a guide to help you

178

California Sushi Roll (Cont.)

roll. Roll up the sushi tightly, allowing it to seal itself with the nori on nori. Slice each roll into 6-8 pieces across, and serve on a plate with a little dish of wasabe, mixed with water, and soy. Garnish the sushi with a touch of caviar or flying fish roe.

Makes 7 rolls, or approx. 42 pieces

* Available at Oriental markets.

Oysters on the Half Shell with Spicy California Dipping Sauce

Purchase small premium oysters, preferably "rack grown" when serving them in the half-shell. They may be opened and served raw, or you may steam, bake or barbecue them until just barely open. Then dip in the Spicy California Dipping Sauce (recipe follows).

Spicy California Dipping Sauce

½ c. rice vinegar
½ lime, juiced
1 t. fresh cilantro, finely chopped
1 t. bermuda onion, finely chopped
1 t. shallot or scallion (finely chopped)
¼ of a fresh jalapeno, approx. 1 t. chopped
   (remove seeds)

Combine all ingredients in a blender or food processor and process until finely chopped. Make 2-3 hours in advance.

Serves 8 as an appetizer

Fresh Pasta with Italian Sausage and a Rainbow of Peppers

Prepare all the ingredients for this dish in advance, before beginning to cook. Have the water for the pasta in a large pot near boiling before starting anything else.

6-8 good quality Italian sausages
1½ c. dry white wine
4 T. olive oil
1 t. red chili flakes
4 garlic cloves, crushed or chopped
3 peppers (1 red, 1 yellow, 1 green), cut into thin, even slivers
salt and pepper
1-1½ lb. fresh spinach spaghetti
4 oz. grated parmesan or asiago cheese

Heat a large pot of water for cooking the pasta. Add 2 T. salt and 2 T. oil to the water. Twenty minutes before serving, place the sausage in a skillet with 1 c. of wine. Pierce with a fork, cover and bring to a simmer. Allow to simmer 10 minutes; then remove the lid and continue to cook, allowing the liquid to evaporate so that the sausage browns lightly on the exterior. *The sauce:* Heat a 10-12" skillet over medium-high heat until a drop of water sizzles on contact. Add the oil, then immediately the chili flakes and garlic. Sizzle that for a moment, but do not allow the garlic to burn. Add the slivered peppers to the pan and allow to cook while tossing and turning for 5 minutes or so, until the peppers are wilting, but

Fresh Pasta with Italian Sausage
and a Rainbow of Peppers (Cont.)

still a little crisp. Turn off the heat and set aside. Add the pasta to the boiling water. Cook and test constantly until it is just tender, from 3-12 minutes, depending on the variety. When it is tender, return the pan of peppers to the heat and drain the pasta. Add the pasta to the peppers and toss very carefully with 2 rubber spatulas coating the pasta with the oil and peppers. Remove the sausage from their pan. Lay them around the edge of a pre-heated oval serving platter and keep warm. Add the remaining ½ c. wine to the sausage cooking pan, and stir to remove the flavor remaining in the pan. Add this to the pasta and sausage mixture; stir and taste for seasoning. Add more salt or pepper or olive oil as desired. Stir in the cheese; then pile the pasta into the center of the pre-heated serving dish and serve.

Serves 6-8

Hot Radicchio Salad with Pancetta* and Chevre

4 oz. pancetta, thinly sliced
4 T. California olive oil
4 T. scallions, finely chopped
2 small head radicchio, washed, dried & torn into bite-size pieces
4 T. red wine vinegar
4 oz. California goat cheese (Chevre)
1 head lettuce, or assorted salad greens
salt and freshly ground pepper

Fry pancetta* until crisp. Remove and drain on paper towels. Discard all but 4 T. of the drippings. Add the 4 T. olive oil to the pan. Saute scallions until soft, then add the radicchio and saute until slightly wilted. Add the red wine and the goat cheese, crumbled. Taste the liquid for seasoning and add salt and pepper as needed. Pour the hot radicchio and dressing over one head of leaf lettuce, torn into pieces, or over your choice of assorted salad greens. Add the crumbled pancetta. Toss and serve.

Serves 4

* A type of ham, available in specialty food shops.

183

Fruit Gratin

1 papaya
1 pt. blueberries or raspberries
6 ripe figs, peaches or apricots
1 c. creme fraiche*, devon cream or sour cream
½ c. brown or demerara sugar

"Gratin" means browned on the top under a broiler. A traditional 10" "au gratin," which is an oval dish that can withstand the heat of the broiler, is the perfect shape for this very easy and fast dessert. Peel, seed and slice the papaya into wedges. Lay them like the petals of a flower around the dish, covering the entire bottom. Next, add a layer of berries, slightly inward from the edge, so that a border of papaya is still visible for contrast. Lastly, halve the figs, or halve and pit apricots or peaches. Lay them on the top in the center. To finish, spread the creme fraiche, devon cream, or sour cream over the top in the center. Sprinkle the sugar over it. To cook, pre-heat broiler until red hot. Place the gratin dish under it, 4-6" away from the heat and broil with the oven door open until the gratin is well browned on top. It is delicious on its own or with vanilla ice cream.

* See Glossary

184

Bed & Breakfast Inns

SWANSON

NAPA VALLEY
CHARDONNAY

PRODUCED AND BOTTLED BY SWANSON VINEYARDS AND WINERY
RUTHERFORD · NAPA VALLEY · CA · ALC. 13.0% BY VOL. · CONTAINS SULFITES

GUEST HOUSE

1436 G Street • Napa, California
(707) 252-8144

This completely restored bed and breakfast establishment was built in 1906 and has lots of charm in its tranquil garden setting. The rooms, with their antique furnishings, private baths, and cheery garden motifs are named Spring Fancy, Summer Garland, Autumn Harvest, Rose's Bower, each with its own individual intimacy and beauty. Brass, mahogany, wicker and beveled glass embellishments are all around, making the Arbor Guest House an inviting place to spend a romantic occasion. A generous continental breakfast is served in the dining room or outside in the garden with home-baked coffee cake, seasonal fruits and much more.

187

Buttermilk Scones

3 c. all purpose flour
⅓ c. sugar
2½ t. baking powder
½ t. baking soda
½ t. salt
¾ c. firm butter or margarine, cut in small pieces
¾ c. chopped dates or currants
1 t. grated orange or lemon peel
1 c. buttermilk
1 T. cream or milk
¼ t. ground cinnamon mixed with
2 t. sugar

In a large bowl, stir or sift together flour, sugar, baking powder, soda, and salt. Cut butter into flour mixture with pastry blender until it resembles coarse cornmeal. Stir in dates and peel. Make a well* in the center of the mixture. Add buttermilk all at once. Stir mixture with a fork until dough cleans the sides of the bowl. Gather dough into a ball; turn out onto a lightly floured board. Roll or pat until ½ inch thick. Using cookie cutter, cut into individual scones. Place on lightly greased cookie sheets and brush tops with cream. Sprinkle with cinnamon-sugar. Bake in 425° oven for 12 minutes or until tops are lightly browned. Makes about 18 scones.

Serves 18

* See Glossary

Apple Nut Coffee Cake

1 c. all purpose flour
1 t. baking soda
½ t. salt
2 c. cored, peeled and diced golden or red delicious apples
1 egg
¼ c. salad oil.
1 c. sugar
1 t. ground cinnamon
¼ t. ground nutmeg
¾ c. chopped walnuts
powdered sugar (optional)

Sift flour, soda and salt together; set aside. Place apple in medium bowl. Break egg over apples, and add oil, sugar, cinnamon, nutmeg, and nuts, blending thoroughly. Stir flour mixture into apple mixture just until flour is moist (mixture will seem dry). Spread in greased 8" square baking pan. bake in 350° oven for 40-45 minutes. Let cool 10 minutes. Sprinkle with powdered sugar if desired. Serve warm.

Serves 16

189

DEER PARK WINERY

Napa Valley
ZINFANDEL

PRODUCED & BOTTLED BY **DEER PARK WINERY**
DEER PARK, NAPA VALLEY, CALIFORNIA, USA
BW 4931 — ESTABLISHED 1891
PROPRIETORS R. & L. KNAPP AND D. & K. CLARK
ALCOHOL 13.8% PER VOLUME

This Zinfandel has a spicy, raspberry nose and full, rich fruit flavors. There is a hint of chocolate in the finish, balanced with oak.

A perfect companion to a wide variety of foods.

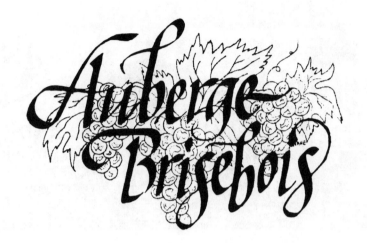

271 Via Monte • St. Helena, California
(707) 963-4658

Overlooking the heart of the lush Napa Valley is Auberge Brisebois, a country-style home with two rooms available for a getaway in the peaceful setting of the wine country. Operated by artist-designer Diane Brisebois Peterson, this private home is set on 5½ acres of gorgeous land with a pool, deck and comfortable living area. With a background in wine-oriented activities and a love of sharing her knowledge with others, Diane is ready and willing to suggest places to enjoy in the surrounding wine country during your stay.

Quick Cinnamon Rolls

1 loaf frozen bread dough (thawed)
1 cube butter
1 c. white sugar
1 T. cinnamon
raisins, nuts (optional)

Roll bread dough out into a rectangle. Pour melted butter over surface. Mix sugar and cinnamon together and spread evenly over dough. Add raisins and nuts if desired. Roll up lengthwise and form a circle, seam side of dough down. Cut ½ through into 2" pieces and twist each piece to its side. Cook at 350° until brown, about 30 minutes.

Serves 12

Auberge Bran Muffins

2½ c. sugar
5 t. baking soda
1 c. vegetable oil
1 qt. buttermilk
4 eggs
5 c. flour (white, wheat or combination)
2 t. salt
1 c. raisins
1 15-oz. box Raisin Bran cereal

Mix everything together. Add Raisin Bran last. Refrigerate 6 hours before using. Bake at 375° for 20-30 minutes, depending on the size and fill of muffin cups or papers. Variation: add orange peel and/or cranberries, trail mix or nuts. Batter will keep 4-6 weeks in refrigerator.

Makes 48-60 muffins

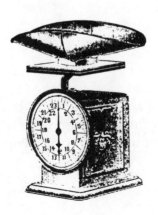

Instead of Crackers

1 roll of 10 buttermilk biscuits (found in dairy case)
4 T. butter
4 T. grated romano or parmesan cheese
½ t. dill weed
   (Variations: minced onion, garlic, poppy seeds, sesame seeds,
   or applesauce and cinnamon)

Put 2 T. melted butter in small loaf pan. Cut rolls in half and
arrange in pan. Sprinkle cheese and choice of seasoning. Drizzle
rest of butter over top of rolls. Bake at 450° for 10 minutes.
Serve with cheese and fruit.

Serves 4-6

Peach Yogurt Scones

2½ c. biscuit mix
¼ c. sugar
1 egg, beaten
½ c. peach yogurt
2 T. butter

Combine biscuit mix and sugar. Stir in beaten egg, yogurt and
butter. Place in greased cake pan. Sprinkle with white sugar. Bake
at 425° for 10-12 minutes. Cut into pie-shaped wedges and serve.

Serves 4-6

Bartels Ranch

**1200 Conn Valley Road • St. Helena, California
(707) 963-4001**

A romantic country inn, set on a secluded 100-acre ranch with the beauty of nature and the outdoors all around, is Bartels Ranch in St. Helena. Innkeeper Jamie Bartels welcomes guests to this country hideaway with three guest rooms, private baths and entrances. Choose from the Brass Room, Sunset Room or Blue Valley Room, each exquisitely decorated and memorable. Your breakfast will be served outdoors on any of the inn's redwood decks, or around the old oak table inside. Wine tasting, a pool and spa are provided for guests to enjoy as they take in the sights at Bartels Ranch.

Bartels Ranch 6-Week Bran Muffins

3 c. sugar
1 c. oil
4 eggs
5 c. flour
5 t. soda
2 t. salt
1 qt. buttermilk
15 oz. box of Raisin Bran

Mix sugar, oil and eggs. Add flour, soda, salt, buttermilk and Raisin Bran. Pour into greased muffin tins. Bake at 400° for 15-20 minutes. Bake as many as needed at a time. Store batter in refrigerator for up to six weeks.

Makes 6 dozen

Walnut Slices

1 cube butter
1 c. flour
2 eggs
1½ c. brown sugar
2 T. flour
¼ t. baking powder
pinch of salt
1 t. vanilla
½ c. coconut
1½ c. walnuts, chopped
powdered sugar frosting (recipe follows)
chopped nuts

Melt butter; add flour to make a paste. Press into 8" or 9" square pan. Brown lightly in a 350° oven. Remove from oven and cool slightly. Beat together eggs, brown sugar, 2 T. flour, baking powder, salt, vanilla, coconut and chopped walnuts. Pour this mixture over cooled paste base and return to oven. Bake for 30 minutes at 350°. Cut into small squares (1") while still warm. When cool, spread with powdered sugar frosting and sprinkle top with finely chopped nuts.

Serves 12

Powdered Sugar Frosting

2 T. boiling water
confectioners sugar
1 t. vanilla

To water, add enough sifted sugar to make frosting the right consistency to spread. Then add vanilla.

Bartels Ranch Coffee

fresh Viennese coffee beans
fresh Sumatra coffee beans
1 T. Mexican vanilla
3 dashes nutmeg

Grind 2 scoops Viennese coffee beans and 1 scoop Sumatra coffee beans. Process in normal coffee maker. Pour 1 T. Mexican vanilla and 3 dashes of nutmeg in bottom of coffee pot. Great treat for the breakfast table.

Serves 8-10

Jami's Famous Garlic Bread

1 loaf French sourdough bread
6 T. butter
1½ c. mayonnaise
1 medium-sized red onion, diced
4 T. garlic salt
1 c. parmesan cheese

Split loaf of bread lengthwise. Butter each ½ of loaf lightly. Mix mayonnaise with red onion. Spread this mixture evenly on both halves of bread. Sprinkle garlic salt evenly over bread. Smother top of bread halves with parmesan cheese. Place on cookie sheet. Broil in oven on middle rack for approximately 10 minutes (until dark on the edges). Serve warm.

Serves 6-8

STONEGATE

NAPA VALLEY
SAUVIGNON BLANC

PRODUCED AND BOTTLED BY STONEGATE WINERY
CALISTOGA, NAPA VALLEY, CALIFORNIA, B.W. 4640
ALCOHOL 12.4% BY VOLUME

Characterized by a hint of apricots in the nose and rose petals on the tongue and in the finish; exceptional raspberry-apricot fruitiness.

Light Pasta entrees, Seafood and especially recommended with cold meat and fish served with fresh fruit.

EST. 1860

BRANNAN COTTAGE INN

109 WAPOO AVE., CALISTOGA, CA 94515, 707 942·4200

**109 Wapoo Street • Calistoga, California
(707) 942-4200**

This beautifully renovated 1860 cottage is a pleasant stop for those who enjoy a refreshing, country look with a keen attention to every detail. Accommodations at Brannan Cottage include six rooms, all with private baths, private entrances, queen-size beds, down comforters, ceiling fans and air conditioning. There is an elegant parlor, furnished in gorgeous velvets with tall windows adorned with crisp taffeta shades. A fireplace and cozy sitting area with complimentary sherry and port is also nice and an afternoon tea is served during the chilly months. All around you'll find lawns and flower gardens with sweet smelling herbs and old-fashioned flowers. Breakfast, a full or expanded continental, is served in the courtyard by the lemon trees. Special events can be arranged, too, if desired, and full catering service is offered as well.

201

Herb Garden Quiche

Pastry:
1 c. whole wheat flour
1 c. unbleached white flour
1 t. salt
⅔ c. butter (very slightly softened)
¼ c. ice water

Sift together the flour and salt. Cut the butter into flour (until pea size). Add the water and stir with a fork until moistened. Form into two equal balls. Roll out into flat rounds on lightly floured surface. Lift gently and place into 2 quiche pans. Trim edge and press into flutes on sides of pans. Prick bottom or crust with fork here and there. Pre-bake at 425° for 5 minutes.

Filling:
2 c. sliced onions
2 c. slices mushrooms
4 T. butter
2 c. milk
2 c. cream
1 lb. gruyere cheese
   (or combine part gruyere and part other Swiss)
8 eggs
2 t. salt
½ t. pepper
2 t. Worchestershire sauce
about 3-4 T. finely chopped fresh herbs
   (basil, rosemary, sage, thyme, parsley, for example)

Herb Garden Quiche (Cont.)

Saute the onions and mushrooms in butter. Drain on paper towel and set aside. Heat the milk and cream until almost scalding. Grate the cheese and add to the milk mixture. Stir milk and cheese until melted and blended. Beat the eggs with a whisk until frothy. Stir salt, pepper, Worchestershire sauce and herbs into eggs until well blended. Add all of this to milk and cheese mixture and stir until completely blended. Place drained onions and mushrooms on pie shells (which have been pre-baked 5 minutes), then pour mixture over this. Bake at 350° for about 45 to 55 minutes. Serve warm or prepare ahead and gently reheat in medium-low oven.

Makes 2 generous quiches.

203

Gingerbread

⅓ cup oil
1 egg
⅔ c. dark molasses
⅓ c. sugar
¾ c. buttermilk
1 c. whole wheat flour
¾ c. unbleached white flour
3 t. baking powder
2 t. ginger
1 t. cinnamon
½ t. salt

Combine first 5 ingredients and mix well. Sift dry ingredients together and add to moist ingredients, using 20 or less strokes to mix. (½ cup of raisins may be added at this time.) Grease and flour an 8" square pan or use individual mini bread pans. Pour batter into pan and bake about 45 minutes at 350°. Do not overbake.

Lemon Honey-Butter Sauce

⅛ c. lemon juice
¼ c. honey
¼ c. butter

Combine all ingredients and warm in saucepan. Pour over the top of individual gingerbread or split piece in two and pour inside.

Jan's Grandma Marion Ross' Scotch Shortbread

1 lb. creamery butter (2 c.)
1 c. superfine sugar
4 c. flour
pecan or walnut halves (optional)

Cream butter; gradually add sugar and cream thoroughly until fluffy at medium speed on electric mixer. Add flour, a cup at a time, until thoroughly mixed. Sprinkle a little flour on a pastry cloth and transfer the dough to pastry cloth. Mix by hand; add a little additional flour until you have one big butter ball. When it starts to split around the edges, stop adding flour. Flatten butter ball out to an oblong shape about 1 inch thick. Cut into small squares and prick with fork in a couple of places on top (prick in a pattern), or roll into small balls or cut into fancy cookie shapes. If desired, press a nut half into center of cookies. Bake on ungreased cookie sheet at 300° for 45 minutes to 1 hour. They should not brown on top and should have just a very slight tinge on bottom. Store in metal container, tighly closed so the butter will not lose its natural flavor. Keeps indefinitely (or at least a long time).

Dry Creek Vineyard™

PRODUCED & BOTTLED BY DRY CREEK VINEYARD INC
HEALDSBURG, SONOMA COUNTY, CALIFORNIA USA

FUMÉ BLANC
Dry Sauvignon Blanc
ALCOHOL 12.9% BY VOLUME

Dry and crisp with hints of herb and citrus flavor.

This wine is extraordinary when served with oysters, seafood
or oriental dishes.

206

B Y L U N D   H O U S E

**2000 Howell Mt. Road • St. Helena, California
(707) 963-9073**

Privacy in a romantic setting, with all the amenities to make your stay a memorable one, can be found at Bylund House in St. Helena. "Modern architecture in the tradition of a Northern Italian Villa" is how owners/hosts Bill and Diane Bylund describe their bed and breakfast inn, tucked away in a secluded valley area with all the activities just a short distance away. The complimentary continental breakfast, air-conditioned bedrooms, private entrances to the guest parlor and lovely balconies help guests feel perfectly comfortable and at home. There is also a swimming pool, spa and courtyard for quiet walks and romantic moments.

Bacon and Water Chestnut Appetizers

2 cans water chestnuts, drained
¼ c. soy sauce
⅛ c. honey
8 slices bacon

Marinate water chestnuts in soy sauce and honey for one hour. Wrap each water chestnut with ⅙ of a slice of bacon and secure with a toothpick. Bake at 450° for 15 minutes; drain and serve.

Makes about 48

Clam Dip

1 8-oz. pkg. cream cheese
3 cloves garlic, crushed
salt to taste
large can minced clams
2 T. lemon juice

Beat all ingredients until well blended. Refrigerate one hour and serve with crackers.

Makes 1 cup

Zucchini Frittata Appetizers

3 medium zucchini, julienned
1 c. flour
½ c. onion, finely chopped
2 T. parsley, finely chopped
1 t. baking soda
1 t. salt
½ t. oregano
2 cloves garlic, crushed
dash of pepper
½ c. oil
4 eggs, beaten
½ c. grated parmesan cheese

Mix all ingredients. Spread in a 13" x 9" greased pan and bake for 25 minutes at 350°, or until toothpick comes out clean. Cut into bite-size pieces and serve piping hot.

Napa Valley

FUMÉ BLANC

Dry Sauvignon Blanc

ALCOHOL 12.5% BY VOLUME

PRODUCED AND BOTTLED BY

ROBERT MONDAVI WINERY

OAKVILLE, CALIFORNIA

The original Fume Blanc and still the natural choice with fish, seafood, poultry and other light dishes.

The Chateau
A Classic Hotel in the Wine Country

4195 Solano Avenue • Napa, California
(707) 253-9300

Combining the warming atmosphere of a country inn and the contemporary conveniences of a first-rate hotel is what Chateau Hotel does beautifully. Located at the entrance to the scenic and famous Napa Valley, The Chateau offers a complimentary breakfast each morning, wine socials (also complimentary in the Hospitality Room), and a one-of-a-kind experience - The Chateau's own hot air balloon, leaving daily from selected spots in the valley. Reservations for a trip across the valley via balloon are available, and the Chateau's friendly staff can acquaint you with many of the other fun-filled sightseeing trips, all within minutes of your hotel.

211

Hot Mulled Wine

1¼ c. water
½ c. sugar
½ lemon, thinly sliced
2-3 sticks of cinnamon, cracked
6 whole cloves
2 whole allspice (optional)
1 bottle (750 ml.) Napa Valley Red Table Wine or
   California Burgundy

Make a syrup by boiling together the first six ingredients for 5 minutes. Strain the syrup and add the wine. Simmer for 15 minutes; do not boil. Keep hot and serve in heat-proof cups with a sprinkle of freshly-ground nutmeg (or bottle, chill and reheat when ready).

Serves 8-10

Orange Fruit Glaze

¾ c. plain yogurt
½ c. sour cream
1½-2 T. honey
½ t. orange peel
sprinkle of nutmeg
4-6 c. fresh fruit (cut up)

Mix all ingredients together and pour over fruit. Serve chilled.

Serves 4-6

Outstanding rich, spicy, fruit nose. Great depth of flavors: rich, but well-defined fruit, some clove and spice. Rich middle with long, lingering finish.

Food pairings: rich fish and shellfish, lobster, crab, scallops and halibut. Cream and tomato sauces, poultry and game birds.

Cinnamon Bear
Bed & Breakfast

1407 Kearney Street • St. Helena, California
(707) 963-4653

At the Cinnamon Bear in St. Helena, you'll find a teddy bear waiting to greet you in every room, and a personal, homey feeling everywhere. There are three double rooms at this unique bed and breakfast house, with individual bathrooms and comfortable bedrooms, affectionately named the Nutmeg, Vanilla and Ginger Rooms. Each has its own private bathroom and air conditioning. The house, built in 1904, has all the charm of home, and lots of teddy bears, and is run with style and care by Genny Jenkins, who makes all of her guests feel like friends. A lavish continental breakfast is served each morning at Cinnamon Bear with pastries and homemade breads.

215

"Bear"ly Benedict

12 split English muffins, toasted and buttered
thinly sliced turkey-ham
1½ c. prepared hollandaise sauce
12 eggs, soft-scrambled with
¾ c. milk
2 T. butter
salt and pepper to taste
paprika
parsley

Assemble the muffins on a large platter, with hot ham on top.
Scramble the eggs; place 1 large tablespoon on top of each muffin.
Spoon hollandaise sauce over all. Sprinkle with paprika for color.
Garnish with parsley.

Serves 8-10

Chili Egg Puff

1 4-oz. can diced green chilies
1 c. grated white cheese (Jack)
1 c. grated yellow cheese (cheddar)
10 eggs
½ c. biscuit mix
1 c. milk
sour cream
mild salsa

In an ungreased 9" x 12" casserole, spread the drained chilies. Add grated cheeses. Place eggs, biscuit mix and milk in blender and process for 15 seconds. Pour over mix in casserole. Bake for 35 minutes in 350° oven. Let sit for 5 minutes to set and then cut. Put dollops of sour cream and salsa on each portion and serve warm. (This is good cold for a picnic.)

Serves 8

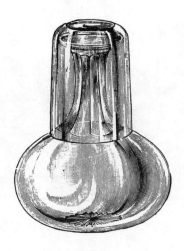

Sweet Buttermilk Biscuits

½ c. sugar
3 c. biscuit mix
1 c. buttermilk
butter

Mix sugar into biscuit mix; make a well* and pour in the buttermilk. Stir until well mixed and forms a ball. Roll onto floured board and work until it is no longer sticky. Pat flat, about 1" high. Butter a cookie sheet. Cut biscuits with a 2" cutter, and position close together on cookie sheet, but not touching. Place a dot of butter on top. Bake at 400° for 12-15 minutes. Serve hot.

Makes 20-24 biscuits

* See Glossary

720 Seminary Street • Napa, California
(707) 257-0789

This elegant, two-story home built in 1852 is gracious inside and out, with lovely European and American antiques adorning each room and a full-size swimming pool and jacuzzi outside. A continental breakfast with freshly-ground coffee, fresh orange juice and homemade croissants and breads is served each morning and, in the late afternoon, a Napa Valley wine is served with cheeses and fruit. Arrangements can be made by the staff for activities in and around the valley, or guests are invited to relax in the parlor in traditionally elegant style.

Cinnamon Logs

1 lb. loaf unsliced, firm white bread (crust removed)
2 c. milk
5 eggs, beaten
2 T. sugar
¾ t. cinnamon
1 t. vanilla
oil for deep drying

whipped butter
maple syrup
6 lemon twists

Cut bread into 4x2x2 inch rectangular logs. Let stand until slightly dry. Blend milk, eggs, sugar, cinnamon and vanilla in a medium bowl. Pour into shallow pan, large enough to hold bread in one layer. Arrange bread in milk mixture, turning to coat all sides. Chill several hours or overnight. Heat oil to 360°. Fry logs in batches until golden brown, 3-4 minutes. Drain on paper towels. Serve with butter, syrup and lemon twists.

Serves 6

Lettuce Bread

1¼ c. sugar
½ c. salad oil
2 eggs
2 t. baking powder
½ t. baking soda
½ t. salt
⅛ t. mace
⅛ t. ginger
1½ c. flour
1½ T. grated lemon rind
1 t. lemon juice
1½ c. romaine or any dark green lettuce, finely chopped
1 c. pecans, coarsely chopped

Pre-heat oven to 350°. Combine sugar, oil and eggs; beat well. Add dry ingredients, lemon rind, lemon juice and mix well. Remove spine from lettuce. Finely chop remaining green leaf part. Add lettuce and pecans to mixture. Pour into greased, floured 9" x 5" pan or two smaller pans. Bake for one hour. Cool ten minutes and remove from pan.

Makes 1 large or 2 small loaves

Golden-Filled Dutch Baby

7 T. butter, divided
3 eggs
¾ c. milk
¾ c. flour
3 Golden Delicious apples
¼ c. almonds, sliced
2 T. sugar
½ t. cinnamon
lemon wedges
powdered sugar
sour cream (optional)

Pre-heat oven to 425°. Place 4 T. butter in a 10'' oven-proof skillet; melt. Put eggs in blender or processor; blend for 1 minute. Add milk, then flour; blend 30 seconds. Pour batter into hot melted butter. Bake in skillet for 25 minutes until puffed. Meanwhile, melt remaining butter in a medium skillet. Pare, core and slice apples; add to butter in skillet, along with almonds. Sprinkle with sugar and cinnamon. Cook until soft and glazed. Cut puffed pancake into wedges and spoon warm apple-almond filling over each serving. Serve with lemon wedges, powdered sugar and sour cream. Serve immediately.

Serves 4-6

Figs, Dates and Walnuts

1 pt. heavy cream
¼ c. sugar
2 c. fresh figs, stemmed and cut in half
½ c. dates, pitted, halved
4 T. Spanish cream sherry
½ c. walnuts, coarsely chopped

Combine cream and sugar and beat until thick; set aside. Combine figs, dates and 2 T. cream sherry. Just before serving, stir walnuts into the date and fig mixture. Stir remaining sherry into whipped cream. Divide fig mixture into 6-8 serving dishes. Top with sherried whipped cream.

Serves 6-8

A UNIQUELY
PLEASING DRYNESS

ELEGANT WINE OF
AND FULL FLAVOR.

EYE OF THE SWAN

VINEYARDS ESTABLISHED 1825

Sebastiani

SONOMA COUNTY

PINOT NOIR
BLANC

PRODUCED AND BOTTLED BY SEBASTIANI VINEYARDS
SONOMA, CALIFORNIA ALC. 13.2% BY VOL.
BONDED WINERY 876

A wine with a copper hue and light vanilla aroma-
full-flavored with a pleasingly dry finish.

A good accompaniment to fish, fowl, light meats, and pasta.

224

BED & BREAKFAST

~~~~~~~~~~~~

850 Conn Valley Road • St. Helena, California
(707) 963-3590

~~~~~~~~~~~~

Tucked away in the lovely woods of the Napa Valley is Creekwood Cottage, a romantic bed and breakfast cottage for two. The newly-renovated suite has its own kitchenette and private bath, woodburning stove and canopy bed. Peaceful and secluded, the cottage is separated from the main house by a jasmine-scented courtyard for privacy. The sounds of the stream as you gaze out onto the grounds from the cottage's private deck make for a wonderful and romantic retreat in any season. Breakfast is served in the cottage each morning and includes many delicious and different selections.

225

Celery Seed Bread

1 loaf of unsliced bread
½ c. butter, softened
¼ t. salt
dash of cayenne pepper
¼ t. paprika
½ t. celery seeds

Peel off top crust of bread and trim crusts from sides of loaf. Cut almost through to bottom crust of loaf lengthwise through the middle and crosswise into 1½ inch slices. With wooden spoon, mix butter, salt, pepper, paprika, and celery seeds. Spread cut surfaces, top, and sides of bread with butter mixture. Bake in a shallow pan at 400° for 18 minutes, or until golden. Snip apart to serve.

Eggplant Pizza

2 T. cooking oil
1 small garlic clove, minced
¾ c. finely chopped onion
¾ c. finely chopped green pepper
4½ T. tomato paste
3 T. water
1 t. oregano, dried
¾ t. basil leaves
¾ t. sugar
salt to taste, if desired
1 medium eggplant
1 egg
1 T. milk
½ c. fine dry bread crumbs
¼ t. freshly ground black pepper
flour for dredging
hot fat for frying
sliced mozarella cheese, anchovies, sliced stuffed
    olives or chopped basil leaves.

Heat the oil in a 1 quart saucepan. Add the garlic, onion and green pepper. Cook, stirring, three minutes or until the onions and green pepper are limp. Add the tomato paste and water. Cover and cook over low heat until very thick, stirring frequently, about ten minutes. Add the oregano, basil, sugar and a pinch of salt two minutes before the end of the cooking time. Remove from the heat and set aside while preparing the eggplant. Wash, peel and cut the eggplant into crosswise slices ½-inch thick. Beat the egg with the milk and set aside. Mix the bread crumbs with the grated

227

Eggplant Pizza (Cont.)

cheese, additional salt if desired, and the pepper. Dip the eggplant slices in the flour, then in the beaten egg, then in the seasoned bread crumbs. Saute the eggplant slices in hot oil until golden, turning to brown both sides. Remove from the skillet and drain on paper towels. Place the eggplant slices on cookie sheets and spread them with the cooked tomato mixture. Top with sliced mozzarella cheese, anchovies, sliced stuffed olives or chopped basil leaves. Place under a broiler until the cheese has melted and is lightly browned. Serve at once.

Serves 2-3

Served as an hors d'oeuvre with wine

228

CULVER'S

A COUNTRY INN

1805 Foothill Boulevard • Calistoga, California
(707) 942-4535

This historical landmark, totally remodeled and restored for guests to enjoy, is a large, three-level Victorian home that welcomes visitors year-round. The rooms are light and open with four upstairs and three down, each decorated in a special way. You can enjoy a sauna and swimming pool at this country retreat, as well as a special breakfast each morning. On Thanksgiving and Christmas, it is Culver's tradition to serve a special holiday dinner with all the trimmings, to its inn guests. Helpful staff members are also available to arrange side trips, dinners, winery tours and more in the Napa Valley for your convenience.

229

Lemon Nut Bread with Lemon Glaze

½ c. butter
1 c. sugar
2 eggs, beaten
grated zest of large, ripe lemon
1½ c. flour
1 t. baking powder
½ t. salt
½ c. chopped walnuts
½ c. half & half

Lemon Glaze:
juice of ripe lemon
½ c. sugar

Preheat oven to 350°. Grease a loaf pan. In mixing bowl, cream butter and sugar until well blended. Add beaten eggs and mix thoroughly. Add lemon zest, flour, baking powder, salt, walnuts and half & half. Mix well. Place mixture in loaf pan and bake for 50 minutes (or until toothpick inserted in center comes out clean). Remove from oven. While hot, spoon Lemon Glaze over bread. Cool in loaf pan.

Makes one loaf

* Lemon Glaze: mix sugar with lemon until completely dissolved.

Mary's Trinidad Grapefruit

½ grapefruit per person
angostora bitters
sugar
maraschino cherries

Cut grapefruit in half and section. Circling center core of grapefruit, lightly pour angostora bitters. Sprinkle sugar on surface of
grapefruit to taste. Place half or whole maraschino cherry in center of grapefruit. Serve chilled.

Scones

2 c. flour
2 t. baking powder
1 T. sugar
½ t. salt
4 T. butter
2 eggs, beaten
½ c. cream
½ c. currants (optional)

Preheat oven to 425°. Lightly grease baking sheet. Mix together flour, baking powder, sugar and salt. Cut in the butter until mixture looks like coarse meal. Add eggs, cream and currants; stir until well blended. Knead mixture lightly into ball. On floured surface, pat down to approximately ¾" thickness, and cut into 12 wedges. If desired, sprinkle lightly with sugar or cinnamon. Bake 10-12 minutes until golden brown.

Serves 8-10

Salmon in Parchment with Vegetables and Mustard

4 T. butter
1 large carrot
1 large celery stalk
¼ c. cream
2½ t. Dijon mustard
4 scallions
parchment paper
12 spinach leaves (washed, deveined, dried)
1½-2 lb. salmon filet (skinned, boned, divided into 4 pieces)
salt
white pepper (fresh ground)

Julienne carrot, celery and scallions. Melt butter, add carrots and celery. Cook about 2 minutes. Add cream and cook down by ½. Add mustard and reduce until almost evaporated. Add the scallions and take off of the heat. Be sure all ingredients are thoroughly mixed. Check seasoning. Butter a piece of parchment. Put 3 spinach leaves down and place a piece of salmon on top; sprinkle with salt and white pepper (fresh ground). Crimp paper to make a pouch. Do this 4 times. Bake in 325-350° oven--15 minutes. To serve, place parchment bundle on plates and cut a criss-cross on top of each.

Serves 4

BLACK MOUNTAIN VINEYARD

ALEXANDER VALLEY

cabernet sauvignon

Fat Cat

GROWN, PRODUCED & BOTTLED BY BLACK MOUNTAIN VINEYARD
HEALDSBURG, SONOMA COUNTY, CALIFORNIA
ALCOHOL 12.9% BY VOLUME

Foothill House

3037 Foothill Boulevard • Calistoga, California
(707) 942-6933

Innkeepers Michael and Susan Clow welcome you to Foothill House, north of Calistoga, in the wooded hills of the country. Each room is decorated with special touches and color schemes focusing on the handmade quilts that adorn the four-poster, queen size beds. Private baths and entrances and small refrigerators, plus a wood-burning stove or fireplace, all add up to a feeling of romance, warmth and comfort as you bask in the natural foothill setting with views of the valley. In late afternoon, a "wine appreciation hour" brings guests together for a complimentary wine selection with cheese, served in the sunroom. The continental breakfast is generous with home-made specialties and fresh fruit.

235

Foothill House Breakfast Drink

1 banana
1 c. plain yogurt
1 c. fresh orange juice, chilled
1 c. hulled strawberries
½ t. vanilla
1 t. clover honey
3 fresh mint sprigs

Blend all ingredients (except mint) in a blender. Pour into 3 large (10 oz.) wine glasses. Garnish with fresh mint. (Note: a teaspoon of Melosa sherry gives a nice "tang.")

Serves 3

Salad with Pecans

1 head butter lettuce, broken
1 can Mandarin oranges, drained
1 6-oz. pkg. pecans, sauteed
1 can French fried onion rings

The above ingredients can be put in a bowl ahead of time, but do not mix.

Dressing:
1 c. oil
1 medium onion
1 t. salt
1 t. dry or wet mustard
7 T. sugar
1 c. cider vinegar
1 T. celery seed

In a blender, mix all salad dressing ingredients, except vinegar and celery seed. Add vinegar and celery seed and mix for 30 seconds. Add dressing to salad and toss to coat as you serve salad.

Serves 6-8

Foothill House "Sweet Dreams"

Note; Foothill House "Sweet Dreams" are left on the bedside table along with a decanter of Napa Valley sherry when turn-down service is done each night.

1 c. butter
1½ c. brown sugar
1 egg
2 c. unbleached flour
1 t. baking soda
½ t. salt
1 t. cinnamon
1 t. ginger
1 c. walnuts, chopped
1 12-oz. pkg. chocolate chips
1 t. vanilla
powdered sugar

Cream butter, add brown sugar and egg and beat well. Mix together flour, baking soda, salt, cinnamon and ginger and blend well. Combine with butter mixture. Fold in the walnuts, chocolate chips and vanilla. Chill for several hours. Form the dough in 1" balls and roll them in the powdered sugar. Place on a cookie sheet and bake at 375° for 8-10 minutes.

Makes 6 dozen

238

Forest Manor

415 Cold Springs Road • Angwin, California
(707) 965-3538

English Tudor charm, secluded woods, fireplaces and a home-baked breakfast all await you at Forest Manor in the hills above St. Helena. With its three stories, spacious air conditioned rooms and tasteful decor, this bed and breakfast spot has many amenities to offer guests. The Magnolia Suite, a one-of-a-kind at the manor, has a mosiac-tiled, double-sized jacuzzi tub and an inviting breakfast area in a windowed alcove overlooking the surrounding forest. The delicous home-baked breakfast is served each morning wherever you choose - on the deck in the outdoor setting, by the fire in the breakfast room, or in your own room for privacy, if you prefer. There are lots of opportunities to take long, woodland walks all around Forest Manor along any of the paths leading through the forest.

239

Bran Muffins

2 c. boiling water
2 c. 100% Nabisco Bran
1 c. oil
4 c. Kellogg's All-Bran
1 qt. buttermilk
5 eggs
2¼ c. sugar
5 c. flour
5 t. soda
1¼ t. salt
2 c. raisins or blueberries

Pour boiling water over the 100% Bran and let stand a few minutes. Add oil, All-Bran, buttermilk, eggs and sugar. Sift together flour, soda and salt. Blend into bran mixture; add raisins. (Batter can be stored in refrigerator for some time.) Pour into muffin tins and bake at 400° for 15 minutes.

Makes 4-5 dozen

Corlene's Granola

1 c. water
1 c. oil
3 t. vanilla
3 c. quick oats
1 c. whole wheat flour
2 c. wheat germ
1 c. sunflower seeds
1 c. cashews
2 c. slivered almonds
1½ c. brown sugar
½ c. sesame seeds
2 c. fine coconut
1 t. salt

Blend first 3 liquid ingredients in blender. Pour into large baking dish. Stir in remaining ingredients. Bake at 250° for 1-1½ hours. Stir often. Store in tightly sealed glass containers.

Makes 13 cups of granola

Corlene's Oatmeal Chocolate Chip Cookies

1 lb. butter
3 t. vanilla
4 eggs
2 c. white flour
3 c. whole wheat flour
2 c. white sugar
2 c. brown sugar
3 c. oatmeal
3 t. soda
1 t. salt
1½ c. raisins
1½ c. walnuts
18 oz. package chocolate chips

Cream together butter, vanilla and eggs. Mix dry ingredients together; combine wet and dry ingredients. Add raisins, walnuts, and chocolate chips. Drop onto baking sheet and bake at 375° for 10 minutes.

Makes 4 dozen

FRAMPTON HOUSE
Bed & Breakfast

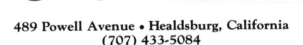

489 Powell Avenue • Healdsburg, California
(707) 433-5084

Attention to detail and personalized service are two of the outstanding qualities of Frampton House, a small bed and breakfast inn with just two spacious guest rooms available. You'll discover a Victorian feeling about this bed and breakfast establishment which features queen size beds, ceramic tile baths and custom designed steeping tubs in each of the rooms. A selection of vintage wines from local vineyards and cheeses are served in the social room and dessert wines are available in the evening. In the morning, you'll enjoy a full country gourmet breakfast in the rustic breakfast room or out by the pool in the more private Japanese-style garden area. Freshly ground French roasted coffee, fresh-squeezed orange juice and many unique breakfast creations are available, and on Sundays, a champagne brunch is served.

Sonoma Jack Cheese Oven Omelette

½ lb. fresh mushrooms
2 T. butter
3 T. chives
3 c. shredded Sonoma Jack cheese
8 eggs
1 c. milk

Clean and slice mushrooms and saute in butter until all liquid is gone. Set aside. Slice chives and set aside. Grate 3 c. Sonoma Jack cheese in food processor and set aside. In a large bowl, beat eggs until fluffy and add milk; beat until smooth. Fold in mushrooms, cheese and chives. Pour into well-greased 9" x 12" pan. Bake uncovered in a 350° oven for 35 to 40 minutes, until mixture is set and top is lightly brown. Remove from oven and slice in six portions.

Serve 6

Blueberry Whole Grain Muffins

1¼ c. whole wheat flour
1 c. quick-cooking oatmeal
2 t. baking powder
1 t. baking soda
½ t. nutmeg
½ t. salt
3 eggs
¼ c. safflower oil
½ c. milk
⅓ c. honey
1 c. blueberries (fresh or frozen)
½ c. chopped walnuts

Preheat oven to 350°. Grease 12 large muffin tins and set aside. Combine dry ingredients and set aside; beat eggs. Add oil; stir in milk and honey and beat until well mixed. Add dry ingredients and beat until smooth. Fold in berries and nuts. Fill muffin tins ⅔ full. Bake about 25 minutes.

Makes 12 large muffins

Potato Pudding

1 large onion, diced
2 c. diced potatoes
2 eggs
½ c. unbleached flour
½ t. baking powder
2 T. diced pimento
1 stick butter
1 c. sour cream

Preheat oven to 350°. Place onion and potatoes into food processor or blender. Blend until it is a fine texture. Add eggs and blend well. Add flour and baking powder, and blend until smooth. Fold in pimento. Pour mixture into 8" greased pie pan. Cut butter into squares and evenly distribute on top. Bake in oven for 50 minutes. Remove from oven and slice into six portions. Serve with sour cream.

Serves 6

GALLERY
Osgood
BED AND BREAKFAST INN

2330 First Street • Napa, California
(707) 224-0100

The beautifully preserved charm of an 1898 Queen Anne set on a lush quarter-acre of trees and flowers awaits you at Gallery Osgood Bed and Breakfast Inn in Napa. Each of the three rooms offered here has its own special warmth and feeling, with names to match - The Lupine, The Poppy and The Rose. Walk through the flower garden, enjoy a view of the surrounding wine country, or just browse around the Inn's inviting rooms in an astmosphere of "casual elegance and home-style hospitality," offered by owners Joan Osgood-Moehrke and Howard Moehrke. Gallery Osgood is also a fine art and craft gallery as well, with unique creations in pottery, glass, wood and photography.

247

Whipped Blue Cheese Spread

3 oz. cream cheese, softened
3 oz. blue cheese, crumbled
½ c. walnuts, finely chopped
¾ c. whipping cream

Cream together cream cheese, blue cheese and walnuts. Whip the cream and fold gently into the cheese mixture. Serve on small French bread rounds or melba toast.

Zucchini and Rice Frittata

2 c. cooked long-grain rice (1 c. raw), cooled
2 c. shredded, cooked zucchini (3 medium), cooled & drained
1 c. olive oil
1 c. grated parmesan cheese
7 eggs, beaten
½ c. green bell pepper, finely diced
½ c. parsley, finely chopped
3 green onions, finely chopped
salt and pepper
2 t. dried oregano

Mix above ingredients in a large bowl. Pour into a 9" x 15" baking pan. Bake in a 400° oven for 25-30 minutes, or until top is golden brown. Remove from oven (any oil still visible will be absorbed). When warm, cut into 1" squares. (Cooked, drained and crumbled pork sausage can also be added.)

Rolled Shrimp Pancakes
with Lemon Sauce

1 egg, beaten
1½ c. milk
2 c. Bisquick
2 c. small shrimp, cooked & cut into small pieces (¾ lb.)
 (reserve some of the shrimp for topping)
1 T. parsley, chopped
1 T. lemon juice
5 drops Worcestershire Sauce
1 dash tabasco
2 T. green onion, chopped
4 T. melted butter
salt and pepper

In a large bowl, beat milk with egg. Add Bisquick and blend. Add all other ingredients except the butter. Add melted butter. Using scant ¼ cup of batter, pour onto hot griddle or into 6-8 inch crepe pan. If using pan that does not have non-stick finish, brush pan with butter first. Cook both sides of pancake and immediately roll it into a cigar shape, serving two to each person. Top with lemon butter sauce (recipe follows).

Serves 8

Lemon Butter Sauce

2 t. lemon juice
8 T. (¼ lb.) butter, softened

Add lemon juice, drop by drop, to butter, beating continually.
Serve with reserved shrimp. *Optional:* Sprinkle top of pancakes
with chopped parsley. Serve with scrambled eggs, sliced
tomatoes, asparagus or green beans.

539 Johnson Street • Healdsburg, California
(707) 433-8140
Specialties: Coffee Cakes, Breads, Frittatas

Each of the seven private rooms at Grape Leaf Inn is named after a grape varietal from the surrounding wine country -- the Sauvignon Blanc, Gamay Rose, Pinot Noir, Cabernet Sauvignon, Merlot, Zinfandel and Chardonnay Suite. The rooms in this 1900 Queen Anne Victorian home are elegantly furnished with lovely antiques, king or queen size beds, oak appointments, and private tiled bathrooms. The grounds at Grape Leaf Inn are well manicured and inviting, as is the full country breakfast served each morning. Complimentary local wines and cheeses are also provided to guests who can enjoy relaxing in the parlor, living room and dining room during their stay.

251

Ham and Tomato Frittata

½ lb. smoked ham, cubed
2 fresh tomatoes, peeled & cut into small pieces
1 small onion, diced
1 T. butter
8-10 large eggs
½ t. curry
salt and pepper to taste
½ c. half and half or cream
¼ c. dry vermouth
½ lb. garlic jack cheese, grated

Grease 7x11" baking pan with butter or margarine. Line the bottom of the pan with ham. Saute tomatoes and onion in 1 T. butter (or margarine) for 5 minutes. Layer mixture on top of ham. Whip eggs, curry, salt and pepper, cream (or half and half) together. Mix in vermouth. Pour egg mixture into pan. Bake in oven at 350° for 25 minutes. Take out of oven and sprinkle cheese on top. Return to oven and continue baking for approximately 10-15 minutes or until eggs are set. Cut into individual pieces and serve immediately.

Serves 6-8 (can be doubled)

Banana/Blueberry Pecan Coffee Cake

½ cube butter or margarine
½ c. brown sugar
½ c. chopped pecans
½ c. butter or margarine, softened
½ c. sugar
1 t. vanilla
3 eggs
1 c. unbleached white flour
1 c. whole wheat flour
1 t. baking powder
1 t. baking soda
1 c. plain yogurt
2 very ripe bananas, mashed
1 c. fresh or frozen blueberries

Grease bundt pan. Melt butter and pour half of butter evenly on bottom of prepared pan. Sprinkle half the brown sugar and pecans in pan. In a large bowl, cream butter, sugar and vanilla. Add eggs. Combine flour, baking powder and baking soda. Add flour mixture and yogurt alternately to sugar mixture, beginning and ending with flour. Add bananas and spread half batter into prepared pan. Sprinkle on rest of brown sugar and pecans. Add blueberries. Spread remaining batter over blueberries. Bake at 350° for 35-45 minutes or until done. Immediately remove cake from pan by inverting onto large plate. Let cool 5 minutes and serve.

Serves 10-12

BAREFOOT CELLARS

GET BAREFOOT TONIGHT

AWARD WINNING VARIETAL WINES
AT POPULAR PRICES!

CABERNET SAUVIGNON	GOLD MEDAL WINNER! UNBEATABLE PRICE
NAPA GAMAY BLUSH	LA FAIR WINNER! TASTIER THAN WHITE ZINFANDEL
SAUVIGNON BLANC	GOLD MEDAL WINNER! SOFT AND FRUITY

Produced by Barefoot Cellars, Healdsburg, CA   (707) 433-8828

Healdsburg Inn
on the plaza

**On the Plaza - P.O. Box 1196 • Healdsburg, California
(707) 433-6991**

Turn-of-the-century style, right down to the claw-footed tubs, antique furnishings and four-poster beds, make the Healdsburg Inn a quaint and enjoyable bed and breakfast inn. Formerly an office building, this beautifully restored inn has private baths, air conditioning, spacious rooms and much more, and is located on the plaza close to the shops in Healdsburg. A hot breakfast with home-baked treats is served each morning on the old-fashioned roof garden.

Orange Frothy

1 c. plain yogurt
½ c. orange juice
1 banana
2 ice cubes

If desired, mix & match additional fruit to equal one cup:
strawberries
seedless grapes
melon
nectarines

Put all ingredients into blender and process for 1 minute until very frothy and creamy. Pour into 12 oz. burgundy glasses. Sprinkle mace on top. Serve immediately.

Serves 4

Lemon Bread

1 c. oil
2 c. sugar
4 eggs
3 c. flour
½ t. baking soda
½ t. salt
1 c. buttermilk
1 c. chopped walnuts
2 T. grated lemon peel
Topping:
1 c. sugar
½ c. lemon juice

Cream oil and sugar together; add eggs, slightly beaten. Mix together flour, baking soda and salt. Beat into mixture, alternately with buttermilk, until smooth. Stir in chopped nuts and lemon peel. Spoon into greased 9" x 5" bread pans. Bake for 1 hour in a 350° pre-heated oven. Cool slightly. Remove from pans. Heat topping ingredients until sugar is melted. Place loaves on pieces of foil. Pour topping over bread. Cool, wrap and store in refrigerator or freezer.

Makes 2 loaves

This wine shows some grassiness in the nose, is somewhat rich and crisp, with hints of oak for complexity.

Enhances veal, chicken or fish dishes.

The Hidden Oak

A Bed & Breakfast

214 East Napa Street • Sonoma, California
(707) 996-9863

The Hidden Oak is a restored brown shingle bungalow built in the early 1900s and located not far from the Sonoma Plaza. Hosts Jacques and Barbara Gasser offer a comfortable and relaxing place to stay at this bed and breakfast inn with a pool, shady veranda and three bedrooms, decorated with select antiques from home and abroad, each with a private bath. The Oak Room, The Farm Room and the Delft Room all have cozy comforters, queen size beds and lovely furnishings. In the morning, you'll be treated to a gourmet breakfast in the dining room. At the end of the day, try the complimentary wine and hors d'oeuvres, served in the relaxing atmosphere of this former parsonage.

259

Fresh Peach Breakfast Cake

2 c. ripe peaches, diced
1 t. cinnamon
2 T. sugar
½ c. margarine
½ c. sugar
2 eggs
1 c. flour
2 t. baking powder
½ t. salt
few drops of almond extract
2 T. sugar

Peel and dice peaches; add cinnamon and 2 T. sugar, stir and set aside. Cream margarine and ½ c. sugar; add eggs and beat until light and fluffy. Stir in dry ingredients and extract. Fold into peaches. Pour into 8" square pan, greased or lined with waxed paper. Sprinkle with remaining 2 T. of sugar. Bake at 350° for 30-35 minutes or until it tests done. Serve warm or at room temperature.

Serves 6

Festive Pears

4 firm pears
½ c. orange juice
1 c. raw cranberries
¼ c. sugar
8 whole cloves
½ t. cinnamon

Peel, halve and core pears. Bring remaining ingredients to a boil. Add pears and simmer gently, covered, about 15 minutes or until pears pierce easily with a sharp knife. Turn pears frequently, but carefully, so as not to mash or break them. Serve pears warm with cranberry orange sauce spooned over them. Drizzle a T. of thick cream over each pear just before serving.

Serves 4

Zucchini Crepes

1 lb. zucchini, pureed
3 eggs
1 T. oil
1½ c. flour
1½ c. buttermilk
pinch of salt
margarine for frying

Puree raw zucchini until smooth. Add eggs and oil and beat again until well blended. Add remaining ingredients and blend well. Using a non-stick pan with the tiniest bit of margarine melted in the bottom, fry 1 crepe at a time, about 1 minute on each side. Makes about 20 crepes, depending on size of pan. Fill with your favorite filling (chicken, ham, cheese, eggs, mushrooms, etc), roll and serve with sour cream. These can be made when zucchini are plentiful and frozen between layers of waxed paper, then wrapped tightly.

Makes 20 crepes

Tuna Platter Hors d'oeuvres

8 oz. cream cheese
3 T. mayonnaise
1 T. horseradish
6½ oz. can tuna
2 T. mayonnaise
2 T. sour cream
2 hard boiled eggs, chopped fine
4 T. sweet relish
1 T. fresh lemon juice
salt and pepper, to taste
parmesan cheese
parsley

Cream together the first 3 ingredients. Shape into a large pancake
about ¼" thick on serving plate. Mash tuna and add next 6 ingredients. Mix well; spread evenly over cheese pancake. Sprinkle
generously with parmesan. Push parsley flowerettes into sides of
pancake to decorate. Serve with crackers or melba toast.

Serves 8

Top Hat Ham

12 oz. spinach (frozen)
½ large onion
20 large mushrooms
1 T. butter
½ t. savory
salt and pepper, to taste
2 T. butter
2 T. flour
½ c. milk
3 T. chopped walnuts
8 portions of ham, sliced about ¼" thick
8 slices swiss cheese
4 egg whites
salt (pinch)

Cook spinach, squeeze dry and chop. Chop onion, slice mushrooms, and saute in butter until mushrooms are dry. Add savory, salt and pepper to taste before completely cooked. Add the 2 T. butter; stir in flour until no longer visible. Add milk and cook, stirring 2 minutes. Stir in spinach and walnuts. Taste for seasoning. Divide this mixture evenly over each ham slice. Lay a slice of cheese over each one. Make a meringue with egg whites and salt and mound on top of each ham and filling. Bake at 500° for 10-12 minutes or until golden. Serve immediately.

Serves 8

The Hidden Oak's Christmas Truffles

½ lb. Baker's semi-sweet chocolate
2 T. brandy
2 egg yolks
5 T. butter
cocoa (unsweetened)

Melt chocolate over low heat with brandy. Remove from heat; beat in the egg yolks and butter. Refrigerate until cool and firm. Roll into small balls, then in cocoa. Keep refrigerated. Makes 25-30 truffles. These are nice left sitting around the inn in bon-bon dishes for guests to share.

265

Hanns Kornell

ALCOHOL 12% BY VOL

750 ML (25 4 FL OZ)

MUSCAT ALEXANDRIA

CALIFORNIA
CHAMPAGNE

PRODUCED AND BOTTLED BY
HANNS KORNELL CHAMPAGNE CELLARS
ST HELENA, NAPA VALLEY, CALIFORNIA

NATURALLY FERMENTED IN THIS BOTTLE / METHODE CHAMPENOISE

**A very dry sparkling wine that is
ususally matched with dessert. Also goes well
with fresh fruit and brunch.**

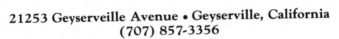

21253 Geyserveille Avenue • Geyserville, California
(707) 857-3356

    Two delightful bed and breakfast inns not to be missed are located in Geyserville, situated right across the street from each other. The charming beauty of the Queen Anne style is brought to life at the Hope-Bosworth House, completely restored and preserved in an elegant and inviting way. Just across Geyserville Avenue is its partner, the Hope-Merrill House, also an elegantly preserved bed and breakfast inn of Eastlake Stick Style Victorian architecture. Both are gracefully and authentically duplicated and preserved homes right down to the last detail - even the wallpaper and trim reflect the period. Relax along the nearby Russian River Wine Trail, stop at the small wineries nearby or just take in the rural atmosphere - whatever your pleasure!

Cheese Souffle Roll

5 T. butter
3 T. flour
1 c. milk, heated to boiling
salt and pepper to taste
grated nutmeg
4 eggs, separated and whites beaten to soft peaks
1¼ c. shredded cheese

In heavy sauce pan, melt 4 T. of the butter over medium heat. Stir in the flour, and when mixture is smooth, gradually stir in the boiling milk. Season the sauce with salt, pepper and a little nutmeg. Cook, stirring, until the sauce thickens, about 5 minutes. Take off heat, stir in the remaining 1 T. of butter. Then add the egg yolks, one at a time, stirring vigorously with a wooden spoon after each addition. Add all but 1 T. of the shredded cheese and fold in the egg whites. Butter a jelly roll pan.* Line the bottom with buttered wax or parchment paper, keeping buttered surface upward. Pour the souffle mixture into the pan, spreading it into a uniform layer with a spatula. Bake the souffle at 350° for 15 minutes, or until is it puffy and lightly golden. Remove the pan from the oven and cover it with a towel big enough to overlap the edges on all sides. Grasp the towel-covered pan and reverse it so the souffle rests on the towel. Carefully lift the pan off the souffle. Allow the souffle to cool on the towel for a few minutes. Peel off the paper lining. The souffle is now ready for various fillings. Once filling is spread, roll up the souffle, using the towel to apply uniform pressure along the rolled edge.

Cheese Souffle Roll (Cont.)

Roll the souffle onto a buttered ovenproof au gratin dish. Carefully slide the roll onto the dish, positioning it so tha the seam side is underneath. Melted butter and the remaining cheese can be put on top of the souffle. Return the roll to a 350° oven and heat for 10-12 minutes or until a light crust has formed.

Variations for fillings: seafood, ricotta, herbs; goat cheese, herbs; sauteed mushrooms; chilies and cheese; sausage combinations; artichokes, cream cheese.

* Jelly roll size pan is 15½" x 10½" x 1".

Serves 4 in ramekins, 6 in roll

Hope-Merrill House
Light Lovely Luscious Pancakes

2 c. flour
2 c. buttermilk (the older, the better)
2 eggs
¼ c. sugar
1 T. baking powder
2 t. baking soda (heaping if buttermilk is old)
1 t. salt
⅝ c. vegetable oil (or melted butter)

Mix all ingredients together and cook on an ungreased griddle at 375° to 400°, turning once. Serve with warm maple syrup, homemade jams or jellies and butter. Also excellent with thin slices of apple, cooked and garnished with cinnamon and sugar. sugar.

Serves 4-6

The Best Gingerbread Ever

1 c. granulated sugar
1 c. molasses
1 c. butter, melted
3 eggs
3 c. sifted unbleached flour
1 T. baking soda
1 T. ground ginger
2 t. ground cinnamon
1 t. ground cloves
1 t. fresh nutmeg, grated
½ t. salt
1¼ c. boiling water
powdered sugar

Pre-heat oven to 350°. Beat 1 cup sugar, the molasses, butter and eggs in a large mixer bowl until smooth. Mix in flour, baking soda, ginger, cinnamon, nutmeg and salt, alternately, stirring in some of the boiling water. Pour into greased, floured 9" fluted tube pan; bake until wooden toothpick inserted in center comes out clean, about 40 minutes. Cool in pan on wire rack for 15 minutes; loosen cake from edges of pan with knife. Invert cake onto wire rack. Sprinkle with powdered sugar. Can be served with a dollop of sweet whipped cream. Delicious!

Makes one 9" tube cake (14-16 servings)

Rosalie's Fruit Muarbataig

Crust:
1 c. butter
2 T. sugar
½ t. salt
2 egg yolks, beaten
2 c. flour

Filling:
6 c. fruit
   (sour cherries, blueberries, rhubarb or peaches)
2½ c. sugar
½ c. + 2 T. flour

Custard:
2 eggs
½ c. cream

In a food processor, blend all of first 5 ingredients together. Press into the bottom and on sides of a 10" tart pan (or 9" x 13" cake pan). Pour in filling, which has been combined with fruit, sugar and flour, over crust. Beat together eggs and cream in custard. Pour over filling. Bake at 350° for 45 minutes. Yield 18 servings (in larger pan). You may have to make adjustments for 10" tart pan.

Serves 18

Rosalie's Favorite
Chili Egg Puff Casserole

10 eggs
1 pt. creamed cottage cheese
½ c. melted butter
1 lb. Jack cheese, shredded
½ c. unsifted flour
1 t. baking powder
½ t. salt
2 4-oz. cans diced California chilies (Ortega Brand)

Beat eggs and add everything else. Bake in buttered 9" x 13" dish or 2 9-inch butter crocks or glass pie pans. Bake for 35 minutes at 350° or until firm and knife comes out clean. Cut in wedges. This can be done and baked just before serving, or even reheated after it has been baked. Mushrooms or spinach may be substituted for the chilies. Enjoy!

Serves 10-12

PRODUCED AND BOTTLED BY FOLIE À DEUX WINERY
ST. HELENA, NAPA VALLEY, CA. ALCOHOL 12.8% BY VOLUME

Medium-full bodied, exquisite blend of fruit and French oak,
lingering finish.

Excellent with all seafood and poultry. Blends well with
lightly spiced foods such as a light curry or mesquite.

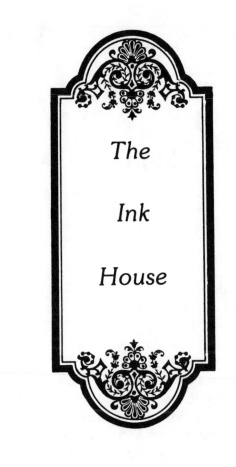

The

Ink

House

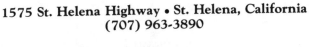

1575 St. Helena Highway • St. Helena, California
(707) 963-3890

Built in 1884 by Theron J. Ink, the Ink House in St. Helena has been uniquely preserved for its guests, with period furnishings, oak, iron and brass antique furniture and even an 1870 pump organ, located in the parlor. You can also enjoy the Ink House Observatory, atop the house which serves as a second sitting room with a 360-degree view of the Napa Valley. Each bedroom has antique furnishings, handmade quilts and lace curtains, plus a private bath. A complimentary continental breakfast of homemade nutbreads, muffins, coffee and juice is served each morning in the dining room.

Muffins

1¼ c. All Bran
1 c. milk
1 egg
½ c. oil
1 c. flour
2½ t. baking powder
½ t. baking soda
½ t. salt
½ c. sugar

Soak bran in milk in mixing bowl for 5 minutes; set aside. Beat egg and add oil; beat again. Then add to bran mixture. Mix dry ingredients in separate bowl. Fold into the bran mixture until moistened. Fill 6 muffin tins 2/3 full. Bake 15-20 minutes at 400°. For variation, add raisins, nuts, dates, apple pieces, cinnamon.

Serves 6

Cheesy Brioche

1 package dry yeast
1 T. sugar
3 T. warm water (110°)
2 c. flour
4 eggs
¾ c. butter, softened
2 c. grated cheddar cheese

Stir yeast, sugar and water into bowl; set aside for 15 minutes to proof. Beat in 1 c. of flour, then eggs; beat for 3 minutes. Add remaining flour and butter; beat well. Stir in cheese (it will be sticky). Put into well-greased 1 lb. coffee can. Cover and let rise for 40 minutes. Bake at 375° for 40-45 minutes. Turn out on rack to cool.

Makes 1 loaf

Pumpkin Nut Bread

1⅓ c. sugar
1 c. mashed, cooked pumpkin
⅓ c. cooking oil
½ c. milk
2 eggs
1⅔ c. all-purpose flour
1 t. baking soda
2 t. pumpkin pie spice
½ t. salt
½ c. chopped nuts

In a mix master, blend first 5 ingredients. Add remaining ingredients; beat at medium speed for 1 minute. Turn into greased 9" x 5" pan. Bake at 350° for 60-65 minutes. Cool before slicing.

Makes 1 loaf

SONOMA HOTEL
1872

110 West Spain Street • Sonoma, California
(707) 996-2996

Built as a two-story adobe in the early 1870s, the Sonoma Hotel has aged with style over the years and is welcoming visitors to its 17 rooms so they too can feel a part of Sonoma history. Located on Sonoma Plaza, you'll find a combination of elegant surroundings, comfort and privacy here as you take in the beauty of this unique hotel. Dine at the restaurant on the first floor, relax at a turn-of-the-century bar with your favorite local wine, or have a look at the many antiques and period furnishings all around. A complimentary breakfast is served each morning.

279

Eggs Albertine

puff pastry (buy frozen)
eggs, poached
Canadian bacon, julienned
Hollandaise sauce (recipe follows)

Roll puff pastry out into an 8" x 14" square, about ⅛" thick. Cut this square into an almond shape, and lighly score the edge of this almond shape, about ½" from the edge. Fold this edge up. Bake at 400° for 15-20 minutes or until brown. Cut off the top of the pastry and scoop out the excess dough. Poach the eggs in 8 parts simmering water to one part vinegar, to desired degree of doneness. Julienne the Canadian bacon and briefly saute. Assemble the poached eggs in puff pastry. Ladle the Hollandaise over the eggs and garnish with julienned Canadian bacon.

Hollandaise Sauce

For every 2 poached eggs, use 1 egg yolk to 2 oz. of clarified butter. Heat the egg yolks, one teaspoon of lemon juice and one teaspoon of water in a double boiler. Whisk continuously until the egg yolks thicken. Slowly add the clarified butter while whipping. Season with salt and cayenne pepper. Assemble the poached eggs in the puff pastry. Ladle the hollandaise over the eggs and garnish with julienned Canadian bacon.

Buckwheat Fruit Crepes

Crepes:
2½ c. milk, scalded
⅛ lb. butter
4 eggs, beaten
1 c. sifted buckwheat flour
1 c. sifted all-purpose flour
¼ t. salt
peanut oil

Filling:
3½ c. hulled and washed strawberries
½ c. water
¼ c. Grand Marnier, Triple Sec or dark rum
large pinch cinnamon
nutmeg, freshly grated
2½-3 large bananas, quartered lengthwise & cut into ¾" cubes
1 c. walnuts or pecans, lightly toasted & roughly chopped

Scald milk and add butter until melted. Let cool slightly; then stir about ½ c. of the milk into the beaten eggs. Pour the eggs back into the milk, whisking constantly. Place the flours in a mixer or food processor. Add the milk mixture slowly to the flours with the machine running, and mix or process just until smooth. Let the batter stand while preparing the filling. *Filling:* many fillings work for these versatile crepes. Use your imagination. (The following is one of our summer favorites.) Finely chop or process ¾ c. strawberries. In a small saucepan, slowly simmer the crushed berries, water and Grand Marnier until reduced by a third. Add spices.

Buckwheat Fruit Crepes (Cont.)

While the sauce is reducing, roughly chop the remainder of the strawberries and cube the bananas. Add them to the sauce, and bring the mixture to a boil for thirty seconds, stirring constantly. Remove from heat; add nuts. This mixture may be refrigerated, but is best used immediately. *For the crepes:* Lighly oil a 7-8" non-stick pan. Swirl ⅛ c. of crepe batter in the medium-hot pan. Let set, then pour off the excess. Cook until just beginning to brown; then turn and cook 1-2 minutes more. Remove the crepe and stack on a warm towel. Fill the crepes with a few tablespoons of the fruit mixture. Roll and serve with whipped cream in the summer, or warmed cream on the cooler days.

Serves 8

Open-Faced Mexican Omelette

Omelette:
2 t. butter
3 eggs, lightly beaten
1 green onion, sliced
1 medium tomato, peeled, seeded, chopped
1 oz. Jack cheese
1 oz. cheddar cheese
½ avocado
fresh cilantro, chopped
sour cream
salsa

Black Beans:
1 lb. black beans, soaked overnight
1 qt. chopped onions
2 T. garlic, chopped
1 T. oil
4 oz. can green chilies
2 c. tomatoes, chopped
2 T. chili powder
2 T. cumin
2 T. white vinegar
¼ oz. oregano
bay leaf
shot of tabasco

Black Beans: Drain the soaking beans and put in an enamel or

Open-Faced Mexican Omelette (Cont.)

stainless steel pot. Add water to cover and boil one hour or until tender. Saute onions and garlic in oil until transparant and add the next 8 ingredients to beans. Simmer 2-6 hours over low heat or place, tightly covered, in a 325° oven for 3-7 hours. (This is enough beans for 10-15 omelettes, but they're a wonderful base for dips or chili, or as a side dish with rice.) *Omelette:* Melt butter in omelette pan. Add eggs and stir with rubber spatula until set but not dry. Layer with black beans, green onions, tomatoes and cheeses. Place in oven or under broiler until cheese is melted. Top with avocado, cilantro and sour cream. Serve salsa on the side.

Serves 2

Red Pepper & Sausage Frittata

3 sweet red peppers, julienned
2 medium red onions, julienned
1 T. fresh garlic (pureed)
8 oz. spicy sausage, cooked, crumbled
1 bunch fresh spinach, washed & cleaned
14 eggs, slightly beaten
salt and pepper to taste
goat cheese (optional)
chopped parsley

Saute peppers and onions until transparent. Add garlic. Transfer
to medium size egg pan. Add crumbled sausage. Spread evenly
and layer uncooked spinach on top of this. Simmer for 10
minutes. Add egg mixture, salt and pepper. Place in hot oven
(425°) for 15 minutes. Then lower the oven to 350° and cook an
additional 25 minutes. Flip the pan (frittata) onto a plate and
garnish with goat cheese and chopped parsley.

Serves 5-7

Pumpkin Bread

1 c. whole wheat flour
1 c. white unbleached flour (sifted)
1 t. baking powder
½ t. baking soda
1 t. salt
¼ c. shortening
¼ c. butter
⅓ c. brown sugar
⅓ c. honey
2 eggs
½ t. cinnamon
⅛ t. allspice
¼ t. fresh nutmeg, grated
1 c. fresh pumpkin puree (seed pumpkin, trim off skin, roughly
  chop and steam in a coverd pan with ¼" water for 1 hour)
½ c. hazelnuts, chopped

Pre-heat oven to 350°. Blend together dry ingredients. Mix wet
ingredients in a separate bowl. Mix wet and dry ingredients, only
to moisten (do not overmix). Fold in nuts. Place in oiled and
floured 4" x 8" loaf pan. Bake for 25 minutes at 350° or until
golden brown and top springs back when lightly touched. Serve
warm with butter or cream cheese.

Makes one loaf

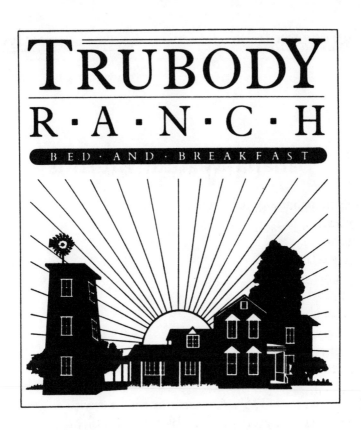

TRUBODY
R·A·N·C·H
BED·AND·BREAKFAST

5444 St. Helena Hwy. • Napa, California
(707) 255-5907

A gothic revival Victorian home with its own water tower and surrounded by 120 acres of family-owned vineyard land, Trubody House was built in 1872 and is an interesting place to visit with its stone milk house, barns and stunning view from the water tower. A breakfast of freshly-baked breads and home-grown fruits in season is served. Breathtaking views of the farm from all of the rooms, and decorations in the style of the Victorian period all make Trubody Ranch a wonderful place to stay.

287

Banana-Walnut Muffins

2 medium bananas (very ripe)
1 large egg
¼ c. honey
1 T. vegetable oil
½ c. yogurt
¼ t. almond extract
1¼ c. bleached white flour
¾ c. whole wheat flour*
1½ t. baking soda
½ c. freshly shelled and chopped walnuts

Pre-heat oven to 375°. Grease muffin tins with vegetable oil.
Combine first 6 ingredients in a blender and blend until smooth.
Stir flours and soda together with a fork in a big mixing bowl.
Pour in contents of blender and stir with fork until batter is just
moistened. Add walnuts and blend with a few strokes. Fill muffin
tins about ⅔ full. Bake 15-17 minutes.

Makes about 1 dozen muffins

* Freshly-ground wheat flour makes a more tender muffin.

Apple Muffins

1 large egg
¼ c. honey
1 T. vegetable oil
½ c. yogurt
½ t. vanilla extract
1¼ c. unbleached white flour
¾ c. whole wheat flour
1½ t. baking soda
1 t. cinnamon
⅛ t. nutmeg
one medium Pippin or Granny-Smith apple, grated

Pre-heat oven to 375°. Grease muffin tin with vegetable oil. Combine first 5 ingredients in blender and blend. In a large bowl, mix flours, soda and spices with a fork. Pour in blended mixture and stir with a fork until just moistened. Stir in apple with as few strokes as possible. Fill muffin tin about ⅔ full. Bake 15-17 minutes.

Makes about 1 dozen muffins

289

ESTATE  BOTTLED

JOHNSON'S
ALEXANDER VALLEY

ALEXANDER VALLEY

PINOT NOIR

PRODUCED AND BOTTLED BY

JOHNSON'S ALEXANDER VALLEY WINES
HEALDSBURG, SONOMA COUNTY, CALIFORNIA
ALCOHOL 12.5% BY VOLUME

A dark red color with a silky texture, this Pinot Noir is excitingly full-bodied. There is a youthful, ripe cherry aroma and a tantalizing full-fruit flavor with a tinge of herbaceousness.

This wine is excellent with lamb, veal and pork. Also, try it with barbecued turkey.

Vintage Towers
BED AND BREAKFAST INN

302 North Main Street • Cloverdale, California
(707) 894-4535

Luxurious suites and beautiful rooms await you at Vintage Towers, located in Cloverdale. With all the privacy you need for a relaxing stay, and all the fun and action the wine country has to offer just minutes away, Vintage Towers is perfect for just about anyone. Choose from several lovely rooms in this Queen Anne Vistorian mansion and enjoy all the comforts of a bed and breakfast inn. Included in the room rate is a generous breakfast, and afternoon refreshments are also provided, compliments of the Weddle Family. Browse through the extensive library, ride a bicycle across the countryside or simply sit back and admire the rose garden from the gazebo.

291

Dan's Berry Good French Toast

Batter:
3 large eggs, beaten
4 T. water
2 c. evaporated milk
1½ t. vanilla extract
½ t. almond extract
1 t. cinnamon
dash of salt

Sauce:
1 pt. sour cream
2 10-oz. pkgs. of the following frozen (or fresh equivalent):
   raspberries, strawberries, blueberries (or any other berry)
   1 t. nutmeg
   1 t. cinnamon

Other Essentials:
1 loaf sweet French bread
2-3 c. Ralston "Sun Flakes" (crushed)
1 cube butter, cut into pats

Best if done the night before: Thoroughly combine the first 7 ingredients; cover and refrigerate. Slice French bread in 1-1½" slices and repack in original wrapping (gives that "day-old" character). Crush the flakes in a sealed plastic bag. Combine the sauce

Dan's Berry Good French Toast (Cont.)

ingredients and store covered in refrigerator. *In the morning:*
Heat griddle to about 325°. Place two slices of bread in batter,
then put a pat of butter on griddle to begin melting. While butter
melts, make sure bread is nicely saturated with batter and coat
evenly with crushed flakes. Brown both sides in hot butter.
Continue process until all pieces are cooked. This French toast
keeps nicely, lightly covered, in a warm oven for 1-2 hours.
Arrange pieces on a warmed plate. Drizzle generously with sauce.
Link sausage and fresh fruit round out this showy breakfast/
brunch dish.

Serves 6-8

Sunday Morning Shrimp Strata

6 slices dill, rye or light rye bread
1 cube butter, melted
8-10 oz. Swiss cheese, grated
4 green onions, chopped
several sprigs of parsley, chopped
½ lb. (or more) cocktail-size shrimp (pre-cooked)
4 large eggs, beaten
salt to taste
2-3 dashes tabasco sauce
1 t. Dijon mustard
2 oz. creamed sherry
1½ c. whole milk
½ pt. sour cream

The night before: Remove crust from bread slices and cut on the diagonal. Dip each piece in the melted butter and arrange 6 of the half pieces in the bottom of an unbuttered 8" baking dish. Spread half the cheese, onions, parsley and shrimp over the bread slices and repeat the process to form a second layer. Thoroughly combine the remaining ingredients, using a food processor or mixer if possible. Pour over casserole, cover and refrigerate overnight. *In the morning:* Bake uncovered at 350° for 50-60 minutes or until a toothpick inserted in center comes out clean. Take caution not to let the edges brown too darkly. Let set about 10 minutes before cutting into 9 equal pieces for serving. This dish keeps nicely, tightly covered with foil, in a warm oven for 1-2 hours. Serve with fresh fruit and fresh baked fruit or nut bread.

Serves 9

Stella's Bread

1 c. vegetable oil
3 eggs
2 c. sugar
2 c. walnuts
3 c. flour
3 c. mashed bananas (or grated zucchini, apple, carrot or combination of any two)
1 t. baking soda
1 t. baking powder
1 t. salt
1 t. vanilla
1 t. cinnamon
1 t. nutmeg

Mix oil, eggs and sugar together. Add all remaining ingredients; mix well (do not overmix). Bake at 350° for 1 hour, 10 minutes or until toothpick comes out clean.

Makes 2 large loaves or 4 individual loaves & 1 medium loaf

ESTABLISHED 1876

Beringer

CHARDONNAY

NAPA VALLEY

PRODUCED AND BOTTLED
BY BERINGER VINEYARDS,
B.W. 46

ST. HELENA, CALIFORNIA
ALCOHOL 13.4% BY VOL.
750 ML

The delicate fruit characteristics of the Chardonnay grape are
evident in this wine, in proper balance with the oak flavors from
partial barrel fermentation and small oak aging. Rich, complex,
and with excellent depth of flavor.

This wine is paired well with a wide range of foods, especially
broiled and sauteed seafoods, chicken and veal dishes. The wine
can stand up to rich sauces as well, adding layers of sensory
perception and enjoyment.

THE
WINE COUNTRY INN

1152 Lodi Lane • St. Helena, California
(707) 963-7077

Aptly named the Wine Country Inn, this small country hotel is situated right in the heart of wine country, two miles north of St. Helena. Fashioned after the inns of New England, the Wine Country Inn combines the old with the new, with each room individually decorated and enhanced by antique furnishings and cozy surroundings. Most of the 25 rooms look out onto the rural area of the valley and a number have vineyard views and balconies. There are no televisions or telephones in the rooms at Wine Country Inn, but there is plenty to enjoy all around you, from the quiet tranquility of the outdoors to the peaceful rush of the Napa River. Each morning, guests awaken to a buffet-style continental breakfast, included in the room rate.

Strawberry Nut Bread

2 10-ounce packages of frozen, sliced strawberries
4 eggs
1 c. cooking oil
1 c. sugar
3 c. all purpose flour
1 T. cinnamon
1 t. baking soda
1 t. salt
1¼ c. chopped nuts

Defrost strawberries. Beat eggs in a bowl until fluffy. Add cooking oil, sugar and defrosted strawberries. Sift together flour, cinnamon, soda and salt into a mixing bowl. Add strawberry mixture and mix until well blended. Stir in nuts. Pour into 2 greased and floured 9½x5x3 or 8½x4½x2½ inch loaf pans. Bake in a 350° oven for 1 hour and 10 minutes or until done. Cool in pans for 10 minutes, then turn out of pans and cool on racks. Makes 2 loaves. This bread slices best then chilled. May be sliced and warmed to serve with butter or sliced thinly and spread with whipped cream cheese and served with fruit salad for lunch or used to make tea sandwiches.

Serves 8-10

Baked Rome Beauty Apples

12 Rome Beauty apples
slightly softened butter *
brown sugar *
cinnamon to taste
ground cloves to taste
walnuts
apple juice

Core the apples, being careful not to core through the bottoms. Trim the tops off evenly. Stuff ½-¾ full with softened butter. Fill the remainder of the core with brown sugar, allowing sugar to coat the top of the fruit. Sprinkle the tops with cinnamon and cloves. Cover the tops with coarsely chopped walnuts. Place in baking dish. Fill the bottom of the pan with approximately ½" of apple juice. Bake at 300° for 45 minutes to 1 hour or until done. Baste the tops with apple juice several times during the baking. Serve warm, topped with half & half.

* Adjust according to the size of the apples

** Variation: before adding butter, insert 6-8 raisins in the core of the apple.

Serves 12

CUVAISON

NAPA VALLEY
CABERNET SAUVIGNON

ALCOHOL 13% BY VOLUME
PRODUCED & BOTTLED BY CUVAISON VINEYARD,
CALISTOGA, NAPA VALLEY, CALIFORNIA, U.S.A.

Created from prime hillside Cabernet vineyards on the western
slopes of Napa Valley, a small amount of Merlot adds to the wine's
deep ruby hue and lushness on the palate.

This is a wine to savor with the finest cuts of beef, a wine that may
be recommended without reservation to the most discriminating
connoisseur.

Sonnie's
Favorite Recipes

1988 American Winery of the Year

Sequoia Grove's Cabernet Sauvignon and Estate-Bottled Cabernet Sauvignon are stellar wines from Napa's Rutherford Bench region. Full-bodied with big, round flavors, they are crafted to enjoy on release or to complement your fine wine cellar.

A perfect match for lamb, roast veal and filet mignon.

302

Asparagus & Cheese Soup

4 T. butter
1 onion, chopped
2 stalks celery, chopped
½ c. white, unbleached flour
6 c. chicken stock
2 T. vermouth
1 lb. asparagus, diced
10 oz. cheddar cheese, shredded
1 T. parsley
salt and pepper to taste

In a stock pot, melt butter; add onions and celery. Cook until soft, about 10 minutes. Reduce heat to simmer and add flour, whisking often (about 5 minutes). Whisk in chicken stock and bring to a boil on high heat. Reduce heat and add vermouth. Simmer for ½ hour. Add asparagus and continue cooking another 10 minutes. Stir in cheese, parsley, salt and pepper and cook until cheese is melted.

Serves 6

English Cheese Soup

½ stick butter
1 lb. onions, sliced
1 garlic clove, minced
¾ lb. potatoes, peeled & cubed
2 c. milk
2 c. water
salt
pepper
4 oz. Stilton cheese, crumbled
parsley, minced

Melt butter in stock pot and add onions and garlic. Cook until soft. Stir in potatoes. Add milk, water, salt and pepper. Bring to a boil and reduce to simmer. Cover and cook for 1 hour. Puree soup; add Stilton cheese and heat until melted. Serve with parsley as a garnish.

Serves 8

Veal Soup

2 T. butter
1 lb. veal, cubed
2 carrots, minced
1 small onion, minced
1 stalk celery, minced
2 scallions, minced
6 c. beef stock or broth
salt and pepper to taste
1 T. parsley, minced

In a stock pot, saute veal in butter. Add vegetables and cook until soft. Add stock or broth, salt and pepper. Bring to a boil; then simmer for 1 hour. Serve with minced parsley on top.

Serves 8

Fried Couscous

1½ c. couscous
2 c. water
3 T. peanut oil
3 scallions, sliced
2 T. ginger root, minced
2 T. heavy soy sauce *
2 T. saki *
1 T. sesame oil *
1 T. toasted sesame seeds
1 T parsley, minced

Combine couscous and water in a ceramic bowl. Microwave on high until water boils. Shut off microwave and let couscous set for 5 minutes. Heat peanut oil in wok and add scallions and ginger root. Cook for 2 minutes; stir in soy sauce and couscous, saki and sesame oil. Sprinkle with sesame seeds and parsley and serve immediately.

Serves 4

* Available in Chinese markets

Broiled Eggplant & Cheese

1 lb. eggplant
2½ T. olive oil
½ t. salt
½ c. Monterey Jack cheese, grated
1½ c. Fontina cheese, grated
2 T. parmesan cheese, grated
4 oz. prepared spaghetti sauce

Cut eggplant lengthwise into 4 slices. Rub each slice with 1 t. oil, sprinkle with salt. Place on cookie sheet and broil for 5 minutes until golden. Turn and broil on other side for 2 minutes. Mix cheeses together and sprinkle on top of eggplant. Return to broiler and broil for 2 minutes longer. Serve with prepared spaghetti sauce, using 1 oz. per slice.

Serves 2

Spinach & Noodles

1 c. egg noodles, cooked
3 T. butter
1 small onion, chopped
1 pkg. frozen spinach, chopped
1 oz. Gruyere cheese, grated
salt
pepper

Mix 1 T. butter with noodles. Melt 2 T. butter in skillet and add onions. Cook until soft. Add spinach and cook for 10 minutes, stirring occasionally. Add noodles. Turn off heat and add cheese, salt and pepper, to taste. Toss and serve.

Serves 2

Acorn Squash with Cranberries

2 acorn squash
4 T. butter
salt
pepper
1 lb. can whole cranberries

Cut squash in half and microwave until soft. Remove seeds. Place
1 T. butter on each squash half and microwave until butter melts.
Season with salt and pepper to taste. Fill each squash half with
cranberries and serve.

Serves 4

Chicken Pecan Salad and Cranberries

1 egg yolk
1 T. cider vinegar
1 T. sugar
½ t. Dijon mustard
salt to taste
6 T. vegetable oil
5 oz. cranberries
3½ c. cooked chicken, diced
3 stalks celery, diced
1 c. pecans, broken
1 head iceburg lettuce, sliced

In a food processor, blend egg yolks, vinegar, sugar, mustard and salt. Let oil drizzle through feed tube. Put cranberries through feed tube, one handful at a time. Mix in chicken and celery. Refrigerate overnight. Mix in pecans and lettuce; toss gently.

Serves 6

Oven-Baked Short Ribs

4 lb. short ribs
3 T. corn oil
1½ c. onions, chopped
2 garlic cloves, chopped
1½ c. tomato puree
⅓ c. lemon juice
2 T. Worcestershire sauce
2 T. brown sugar
2 T. Dijon mustard
2 T. red wine vinegar
salt and pepper to taste
1 T. minced parsley
buttered noodles

Brown ribs in a large skillet in oil. Turn ribs once and brown other side. Transfer to a large casserole. In same skillet, add onions and garlic and cook for 3 minutes, stirring often. Add tomato puree, lemon juice, Worcestershire sauce, sugar, mustard, vinegar, salt and pepper and mix well. Cook for 5 minutes and pour over short ribs. Bake at 325° for 3 hours, turning the ribs every ½ hour. Sprinkle with parsley and serve over noodles.

Serves 6

Oriental Chicken

¼ c. rice vinegar *
¼ c. sugar
¼ c. soy sauce
2 lbs. chicken thighs
2 garlic cloves, minced
1 T. ginger, minced

Combine vinegar, sugar and soy sauce. Place chicken in plastic bag and add combined sauce. Marinate overnight in refrigerator. Heat a large skillet and add marinated chicken. Add garlic and ginger and bring to a boil. Reduce to simmer, cover and cook for 15 minutes. Uncover and cook for 15 more minutes. Remove chicken and reduce sauce until thick. Place chicken back into skillet to coat with sauce. Serve over steamed oriental rice.

Serves 4

* Available in Oriental markets

Chicken Marmalade

⅓ c. white unbleached flour
½ t. salt
¼ t. pepper
8 chicken thighs
1½ T. oil
¾ c. orange juice
2 T. soy sauce
1 t. ginger, minced
¼ c. marmalade

Combine flour, salt and pepper in a dish. Dredge chicken in flour mixture. In a large skillet, heat oil and add chicken. Cook on high heat for 10 minutes, turning once. Add orange juice, soy sauce and ginger. Cover and simmer for 45 mintues. Stir in marmalade and simmer for 5 more minutes. Serve over a bed of wild rice.

Serves 4

Chocolate Raisin Lemon Cookies

3 eggs
2 c. light brown sugar
1 c. corn oil
zest from 1 lemon
⅓ c. lemon juice
1 t. lemon extract
2 c. unbleached white flour
1 t. baking soda
1 t. salt
1½ c. oatmeal
1 c. golden raisins
1 c. chocolate chips

In a food processor, beat the eggs and sugar. Add oil, lemon zest, juice and extract. In a bowl, sift together flour, soda and salt and add it to the egg mixture. Then add the oatmeal. Stir in raisins and chocolate chips. Drop by tablespoonful, 2" apart, onto buttered baking sheet. Bake at 350° for 15 minutes.

Makes about 3 dozen cookies

Glossary

BECHAMEL SAUCE - Cook 1½ c. stock with 1 slice onion, 1 slice carrot, 1 bay leaf, sprig of parsley and 6 peppercorns; strain. Melt ¼ c. butter, add ¼ c. flour and gradually add hot stock and 1 c. scalded milk. Add ½ t. salt and ⅛ t. pepper.

BEURRE BLANC - A warm, thick, creamy and butter-colored sauce.

BLANCH - To briefly heat foods in a large quantity of boiling water and sometimes placed in ice water afterwards to stop the cooking process.

BRAISE - To sear meat over high flame in oil and then cook slowly in an oven in a covered dish with a small quantity of liquid.

BROWN SAUCE (quick) - Bring 2 c. beef stock to a boil and then simmer for 15 minutes. Add 2 t. cornstarch or arrowroot dissolved in 3 T. cold water and cook over moderate heat, stirring constantly, until thickened. Then simmer for 5 minutes.

CLARIFIED BUTTER - Heat whole butter very slowly. Remove white deposit that forms on top. Strain the butter through a sieve into a small bowl, leaving the milky solids in the bottom of the pan. Store uncovered in refrigerator, as it will keep indefinitely.

CREME ANGLAISE - Beat 6 egg yolks and add ⅓ c. sugar, 1 T. at at time. Add a pinch of salt. Whisk until mixture ribbons when the whisk is lifted. Add 2 c. scalded milk and keep whisking. Transfer to saucepan and cook over moderate heat, whisking until thick. Remove from heat and stir in 2 t. vanilla. Strain custard in small bowl. Set in larger bowl filled with cracked ice and let cool. Stir; chill the sauce, covered.

CREME FRAICHE - Heavy cream that has been allowed to ferment slightly. To make your own, combine 2 parts heavy cream to 1 part sour cream or buttermilk. Cover bowl and set out at room temperature about 4 hours. Then refrigerate until ready to use.

Glossary (Cont.)

DEGLAZE - Pour wine into pan in which food has been prepared in butter (food has been removed and just the pan juices remain).

EGG WASH - 1 egg beaten with 1 T. water.

HOLLANDAISE SAUCE - Divide ½ c. butter into 3 pieces. Put 1 piece in double boiler with 2 egg yolks and 1 T. lemon juice. Stir constantly with a whisk until butter is melted. Add second piece of butter and then third piece. Add ⅓ c. boiling water and ¼ t. salt.

MIRE POIX - Mixture used in meat, fish and shellfish dishes to enhance their flavor.

ROUX - Mixture of butter and flour. Melt butter in saucepan, add flour slowly and whisk until thick.

SEAR - To brown surface of meat quickly with high heat.

WATER BATH - Place the recepticle in which you are cooking the ingredients into a large recepticle, to which an amount of water has been added.

Index

A

B

D

E

F

G

H

I

J

L

M

O

P

Q

R

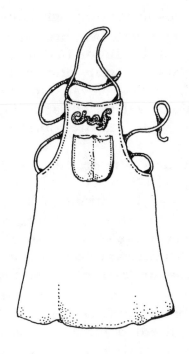

About the Author

Sonnie Imes, a native of Philadelphia, Pa., has lived in Incline Village, Nevada on the North Shore of Lake Tahoe for the past eight years. Her interest in cooking began when she was tall enough to reach the sink and clean up her own dishes.

Sonnie considered her Dad her best critic and audience-always willing to try her new concoctions. She has even been able to transform her husband, Dick Imes' palate into a gourmet one - even though he is a confirmed meat and potatoes man.

A gourmet cook in her own right, this is her sixth book, the other five featuring favorite recipes of renowned restaurants in the Lake Tahoe Basin, Reno and Marin.

Sonnie has always been an innovator. Twelve years ago while living in Las Vegas, Nevada, she wrote an article for the *Nevada Times* on a dare. The article was such a success that it became a regular feature column until she left the area.

In Incline Village, she produces and directs her own television show on PBS, called "A *Taste of Tahoe*," featuring chefs from area restaurants who prepare gourmet treats on the air. Sonnie is also teaching two cooking classes for Sierra Nevada College - one on using the food processor and the other on microwave cooking, as well as Chinese cooking classes for the Incline Village Recreation Dept.

Among her other interests (when she's not busy proving recipes or creating her own) are all kinds of handiwork, including needlepoint, knitting, stained glass and macrame. She also enjoys reading and skiing.

In the works now are several other cookbooks, including "The Tastes of Hawaii," "The Tastes of San Fransisco," "The Tastes of Carmel/Monterey," and possibly "The Tastes of New England."

Cover Photo: Mary Rasmussen

Typesetting & Layout: The Tahoe Supersaver

Literary Comments & Proofreading: Kim Zaski

Printing: Publisher's Press

For comments, re-orders, the address of your nearest distributor, or information on starting a restaurant guide for your city, please contact:

The Tastes of Tahoe
P.O. Box 6114
Incline Village, NV 89450
(702) 831-5182

GEYSER PEAK WINERY

WELCOME TO OUR TASTING ROOM...

*The tasting room carries special bottlings, older
vintages and rare varieties unavailable elsewhere:*

- **Cabernet Franc**
- **Malbec**
- **Estate Reserve
Chardonnay**

- **Estate Reserve
Cabernet Sauvignon**
- **Reserve Alexandre
and many others.**

GEYSER PEAK WINERY

HWY. 101

ALEXANDER VALLEY

CANYON ROAD

GEYSERVILLE

DRY CREEK VALLEY

HWY. 128 TO NAPA VALLEY

HWY. 101

ALEXANDER VALLEY RD.

HEALDSBURG

WINDSOR

SANTA ROSA

TO SONOMA VALLEY

HWY. 12

OPEN DAILY 10 AM TO 5 PM

NO CHARGE
FOR TASTING

*Located 85 scenic miles
north of San Francisco
in Sonoma County's famed
Alexander Valley.
Take the Canyon Road
exit from HIghway 101*

*PICNIC
FACILITIES*

GEYSER PEAK WINERY • 22281 Chianti Road • Geyserville, CA 95441
FAX 707-857-3545 • Tel. 707-433-6585 • Toll Free 1-800-255-WINE (CA ONLY)

THE TASTES Of TAHOE

SONNIE IMES
P.O. BOX 6114
INCLINE VILLAGE, NV 89450
702 / 831-5182

Please send_____copies of THE TASTES OF CALIFORNIA WINE
COUNTRY -NAPA/SONOMA @ $11.95 each

Please send_____copies of THE TASTES OF CALIFORNIA WINE
COUNTRY -NORTH COAST @ $11.95 each

Please send_____copies of THE BEST OF THE TASTES OF TAHOE @
$11.95 each

Please send_____copies of THE TASTES OF CRUISING @ $11.95 each

Add $2.00 postage and handling for the first book ordered and $.50 for each
additional book. Enclosed is my check for $_____

Name_____

Address_____

City_____State_____Zip_____

This is a gift. Send directly to:
Name_____

Address_____

City_____State_____Zip_____

Autographed by author.

Autographed to:_____

THE
MEEKER
VINEYARD

ESTATE BOTTLED
ZINFANDEL
DRY CREEK VALLEY · SONOMA COUNTY

CHARLES R. MEEKER, WINEMAKER

GROWN, PRODUCED AND BOTTLED BY THE MEEKER VINEYARD
9711 WEST DRY CREEK ROAD, HEALDSBURG, CALIFORNIA
CONTAINS SULFITES · ALCOHOL 13.4% BY VOLUME

THE TASTES Of TAHOE

SONNIE IMES
P.O. BOX 6114
INCLINE VILLAGE, NV 89450
702 / 831·5182

Please send_____copies of THE TASTES OF CALIFORNIA WINE
COUNTRY -NAPA/SONOMA @ $11.95 each

Please send_____copies of THE TASTES OF CALIFORNIA WINE
COUNTRY -NORTH COAST @ $11.95 each

Please send_____copies of THE BEST OF THE TASTES OF TAHOE @
$11.95 each

Please send_____copies of THE TASTES OF CRUISING @ $11.95 each

Add $2.00 postage and handling for the first book ordered and $.50 for each
additional book. Enclosed is my check for $_____

Name_____

Address_____

City_____State_____Zip_____

This is a gift. Send directly to:
Name_____

Address_____

City_____State_____Zip_____

Autographed by author.
Autographed to:_____

Notes

Notes

Notes

Notes

ROBERT STEMMLER WINERY

SONOMA COUNTY
PINOT NOIR
Alcohol 12.8% by Volume

This wine is of the new generation of Pinot Noir from the Golden State that offers the lush fruitiness, silky texture and complex aromas of the best Burgundies.

Stemmler's Pinot Noir is very popular with restaurateurs throughout the United States because it has such a wide affinity with different foods, particularly lighter dishes such as seafood, fowl, veal and pork.